AMERICAN HORTICU
PRACTICAL GUIDES

SMALL
TREES

D0362626

AMERICAN HORTICULTURAL SOCIETY PRACTICAL GUIDES

SMALL TREES

ALLEN J. COOMBES

DORLING KINDERSLEY PUBLISHING, INC.
www.dk.com

DORLING KINDERSLEY PUBLISHING, INC.
www.dk.com

PRODUCED FOR DORLING KINDERSLEY BY STUDIO CACTUS,
13 Southgate Street, Winchester, Hampshire

PROJECT EDITOR Polly Boyd
PROJECT ART EDITOR Ann Thompson

SERIES EDITOR Gillian Roberts
SERIES ART EDITOR Stephen Josland
US EDITOR Ray Rogers

SENIOR MANAGING EDITOR Mary-Clare Jerram
MANAGING ART EDITOR Lee Griffiths

DTP DESIGNER Louise Paddick

PRODUCTION CONTROLLER Mandy Inness

First American Edition, 2000
2 4 6 8 10 9 7 5 3 1

Published in the United States by
Dorling Kindersley Publishing, Inc., 95 Madison Avenue, New York, NY 10016

Dorling Kindersley Publishing, Inc. offers special discounts for bulk purchases for sales promotions or
premiums. Specific, large-quantity needs can be met with special editions, including personalized covers,
excerpts of existing guides, and corporate imprints
For more information, contact Special Markets Department, Dorling Kindersley
Publishing, Inc., 95 Madison Avenue, New York, NY 10016 Fax: 800-600-9098

Library of Congress Cataloging-in-Publication Data

Small trees. -- 1st American ed.
    p. cm. -- (AHS practical guides)
    Includes index.
    ISBN 0-7894-5070-4 (pbk. : alk. paper)
    1. Ornamental trees. I. DK Publishing, Inc. II. American
    Horticultural Society. III. Series.
SB435.S57 1999
635.9'771--dc21   99-41067
                                                      CIP

Reproduced by Colourscan, Singapore
Printed and bound by Star Standard Industries, Singapore

CONTENTS

WHY HAVE SMALL TREES? 7

How to use small trees creatively to provide structure
and interest in small areas.

PLANTING AND TREE CARE 41

How to plant and care for trees so that they give their best
display; pruning young and mature trees.

RECOMMENDED SMALL TREES 61

The best trees to grow in small spaces.

WHY HAVE SMALL TREES?

WHAT IS A TREE?

TREES ARE GENERALLY THE LARGEST and most prominent of garden plants. They are usually defined as woody plants that will grow on a single stem to at least 15–20ft (5–6m) tall, whereas a shrub, which is also woody, is normally lower growing, with several or many stems from the base. However, there is not always a clear division between the two; some plants that we think of as trees can be shrubby, while some shrubs can develop a treelike habit.

TREES IN SMALL SPACES

While many trees are vast, a great number are more modest in stature and are ideally suited to small areas. Most of the trees featured in this book reach only about 30ft (10m) tall; however, some taller, narrow trees are also included, since they are useful where the width rather than the height of tree is the limiting factor. Many trees grow well in containers (*see pp.32–35*) and are ideal for enlivening paved areas such as roof terraces, patios, and courtyards.

BENEFITS OF TREES

- Trees are highly ornamental plants. They add form, height, and structure to garden areas.
- They can be used to create focal points, to highlight or hide parts of a garden, or to frame or obscure the outside world.
- Trees are long-lived, and they require little attention once they are established.
- They encourage wildlife in their branches, on their bark, and on the ground beneath.
- Trees can provide shelter and shade.

SPRING-FLOWERING CHERRY *Throughout the year, trees bring color, form, and substance to an area: many offer glorious flowers and foliage in spring and summer (here,* Prunus 'Hally Jolivette'), *magnificent color in autumn, and striking, bare-branched silhouettes in winter. Trees make a bold statement in their own right; they also complement other plantings and create sheltered or shady areas in which to grow many other plants.*

◄AUTUMN GLORY *Ablaze with color, this cherry is offset dramatically by the bluish green conifer.*

TREES IN PLANTING PLANS

The size and layout of your property will determine the number of trees to plant and their positions. In a very small space, there may be only enough space for one tree and little choice of where to plant it. As the size of the space increases, so do the possibilities of using trees in design.

Some trees make excellent specimen plants. They may form an eye-catching focal point or may highlight an area by drawing attention to it. Many combine well with other plantings. The mixed

---

Trees may be used to highlight or hide certain areas

---

border – an important feature in many small properties – combines both woody and herbaceous plants. Here, trees combine happily with shrubs and perennials and lend height, structure, and year-round interest to any display.

It may be necessary to change the planting around a tree as it grows, using sun-loving plants around a young tree and

BRIGHTENING A DARK AREA
Shade-tolerant plants, such as the maple Acer shirasawanum *'Aureum' and* Pittosporum *'Garnettii', can lighten a shady corner.*

changing them for shade-tolerant ones as the tree spreads and creates more shade. An alternative approach is to grow an upright tree that will cast little shadow, for example the cherry *Prunus* 'Amanogawa' or *Thuja occidentalis* 'Smaragd', or to underplant shrubs that will grow well in both sun and shade, such as *Euonymus fortunei* cultivars or hydrangeas.

Before planting a tree, there are various important points to consider that will effect the kind of tree you plant and its position. First, decide whether you wish to retain a given view or to obscure it. Trees can do both effectively: they may conceal a nearby building or frame a view to distant hills.

A TREE AS A FOCAL POINT
Viewed through an archway in the hedge, this carefully placed crabapple, Malus *'Golden Hornet', is a striking and effective focal point.*

Consider whether you want the tree to divide an area, creating a screen between two distinct areas, or to draw the eye into another area. The tree's ornamental features should also have a bearing on its position. If you are growing a tree for its bark, it needs to be in a reasonably open position where the bark can be seen to best effect, whereas one grown for its spring flowers or autumn color could

> ## If space is at a premium, select a tree with two or more seasons of interest

be planted among shade-tolerant shrubs and still get noticed. Never be tempted to plant a tree that will become too large for the site. In the majority of cases, it is impractical as well as undesirable to prune most trees to restrict their size.

In a small space, avoid planting too many yellow-leaved, variegated, or purple-leaved

YEAR-ROUND INTEREST
Many trees are ornamental over several seasons. The crabapple Malus 'Red Sentinel' offers spring flowers and fruits into winter.

trees. While they are useful for highlighting and drawing attention to certain parts of your property, they can dominate in a central position. Trees with bold foliage or a strong, upright habit are often very effective near buildings.

Where there is space for only one or two trees, the ornamental features are especially important. A wide range of trees has attractions that span two or more seasons – flowers, then autumn color, and attractive bark, for example – so these are a good choice for very small spaces, where every plant must earn its keep. Many trees are attractive throughout the year. Birches, for example, bear their fresh green leaves and catkins in spring; the elegantly drooping foliage in summer turns to yellow in autumn; and the striking white bark is a particularly welcome feature in winter.

SUITING THE TREE TO THE SITE

ALTHOUGH MANY TREES will grow happily in a range of garden conditions, there are those that prefer or even require a certain position or soil type. If you wish to plant a particular tree, make sure you can provide the conditions that enable it to thrive. Remember to take into account practical factors such as space available, exposure to wind, amount of shade, and whether the soil is dry, moist, acidic, or alkaline (see p.42).

SUN AND SHADE

Most trees will tolerate a fairly broad range of conditions from full sun to partial shade and will succeed where they are shaded by a building or other trees for several hours of the day. Others, however, will positively thrive in full sun, flowering and growing the better for it. Most trees with colored or variegated foliage are at their best if given plenty of light, but they do not necessarily need full sun all day. If grown in too much shade, their foliage tends to become greener and less interesting.

With some trees, it is a case of balancing the plant's requirements. The very beautiful beech, *Fagus sylvatica* 'Aurea Pendula', for

▲ SUN-LOVING BUDDLEJA
Buddleja alternifolia, *grown as a weeping standard, is an ideal small tree for a sunny position. Fewer fragrant, early summer flowers would be produced in a shadier site.*

◄ SHADE-TOLERANT STYRAX
Naturally a woodland species, the graceful, spreading Japanese snowbell tree (Styrax japonicus) *will flower well and produce good autumn color in shady sites in the garden.*

example, has bright yellow foliage, which may burn in full sun when it emerges; it is therefore best given a bright position among other trees. In the case of the sour-wood (*Oxydendrum arboreum*) and *Stewartia pseudocamellia*, both full sun and a moist soil are needed. If these conditions are difficult to provide, then such trees are best grown in partial shade, where the soil is likely to be moister.

> ## Most trees with variegated leaves perform best in plenty of light

Some trees grow well in light shade, either under larger trees or where they are prevented from receiving sun for most of the day, for example in the shadow of a building. The area beneath a large, densely leafy tree may be very dry as well as shady, so grow trees that tolerate dry, shady sites, such as hollies (*Ilex*) and snowbells (*Styrax*), or add a soil improver before planting.

SUN-WORSHIPPING CERCIS
The Judas tree (Cercis siliquastrum) *originates in the hot, sunny climate of the eastern Mediterranean. If given a site in full sun, it bears a profusion of pink flowers in spring.*

WHICH TREE WHERE?

TREES FOR SUNNY SITES
Acer griseum
Crataegus
Franklinia alatamaha
Koelreuteria paniculata
Magnolia
Malus
Prunus
Pyrus
Syringa reticulata

TREES FOR SHADY SITES
Acer (many)
Amelanchier
Carpinus
Ilex
Ostrya virginiana
Photinia
Styrax japonicus

TREE SHAPES

THE SHAPE OF A TREE has a major impact, especially in a small area. For most of the year, a tree will not be in flower or fruit or showing autumn color, so it is the form that, to a great extent, sets the mood and style. When selecting a tree, always consider the shape as well as the ultimate height. If horizontal space is restricted, conical or columnar trees are best, since they occupy less space than spreading trees of the same height.

COLUMNAR TREES

Trees defined as "columnar" are upright, with an ultimate height greater than their spread; the crown is more or less parallel-sided. The broadest of these, which may be only a little taller than wide, are often called "broadly columnar," the narrowest are classified as "narrowly columnar."

The columnar habit has distinct advantages in small spaces. A tree of relatively narrow spread takes up less space, enabling it to be grown in more confined areas than a wider-spreading tree. In addition, the fact that a columnar tree creates less shade allows a greater range of plants to be grown beneath it.

One of the great characteristics of columnar trees is that they create a bold statement, which makes them excellent as focal points or specimen trees. With their distinctive shape, they stand out beautifully and complement both trees and shrubs of more spreading habits.

▲ LOLLIPOP-SHAPED SPECIMEN
The hornbeam Carpinus betulus *'Columnaris' makes a strong, bold statement in this setting. These trees are narrowly columnar when young, becoming more rounded with age.*

BROADLY COLUMNAR   NARROWLY COLUMNAR   BROADLY CONICAL   NARROWLY CONICAL

CONICAL TREES

Conical trees are similar to columnar trees in that they are upright, with a height that is greater than their spread. They differ, however, in that their crowns are not parallel-sided but instead are tapered to a point. As with columnar trees, the ratio of height to spread varies considerably, with the broadest termed "broadly conical," and the more slender and spirelike classified as "narrowly conical." Because of their distinctive habit, conical trees make good specimen trees or focal points and are also

> In confined spaces,
> upright forms are better
> than spreading shapes

effective in mixed borders, where they provide interesting, contrasting shapes.

Narrow trees can often be used effectively in groups or pairs. A group of three slender trees, such as *Pinus sylvestris* 'Fastigiata', makes a bold feature and can occupy less space than a single spreading tree. Narrow trees can also be used to flank a path or gateway, with little danger of obstruction as they grow. Alternatively, they can frame a view from an area or, together with other trees of similar shape, form an effective component of a screen.

▲ CONICAL CONIFER
Chamaecyparis
obtusa '*Crippsii*', a
*good specimen tree,
is tall and slender
when young but
becomes broader and
more open with age.*

◀ TREE SHAPES
*Trees come in a wide
range of forms. The
shape of the tree you
choose will influence
which plants you can
grow beneath it.*

ROUNDED TO BROADLY SPREADING   WEEPING

ROUNDED TO SPREADING TREES

Trees that are defined as "rounded to spreading" have a crown that is generally broader than it is tall. These are very attractive in form, but they take up more horizontal space than upright trees.

When choosing a tree, always check on its eventual shape. In the nursery, many young

---

Many young trees are upright but become wide-spreading with age

---

trees have an upright habit, which several years later will start to spread widely. Take care at planting to ensure that trees of a spreading habit will not later encroach on other plants or structures. Also, consider

WEEPING CHERRY
The elegant habit of this cherry, Prunus pendula *'Pendula Rosea', is offset by a dark background of upright evergreens, which form an excellent foil for the pink flowers.*

your choice of plants beneath the tree. Spreading trees produce the largest areas of shade, some light and dappled, others dense. Those that create dense shade are useful for screening and naturally provide the ideal conditions for growing shade-loving plants (*see p.37*).

WEEPING TREES

Weeping trees are usually spreading in habit, with pendulous branches, although some, such as the beech *Fagus sylvatica* 'Aurea Pendula', retain a narrow form.

One kind of weeping tree is particularly useful for small gardens. Plants that would naturally grow as low, spreading mounds close to the ground are instead grafted on top of a stem at about 4–6ft (1.2–2m) tall. When grown in this way, the normally creeping shoots arch gracefully to the ground, creating a weeping tree. Examples of some good weeping standards include *Caragana arborescens* 'Pendula', *Cotoneaster* 'Hybridus Pendulus', and the cherry *Prunus* 'Kiku-shidare-zakura'.

◀ BROADLY CONICAL
Conical trees, such as the crab-apple Malus tschonoskii, *stand out well among other trees of contrasting shapes.*

▼ SHRUB GROWN AS A TREE
The willow Salix integra *'Hakuro-nishiki' is a shrub that is usually grafted on a stem to make a small tree.*

TREES WITH DISTINCTIVE SHAPES

BROADLY COLUMNAR
Acer palmatum 'Shishigashira'
Aesculus × *neglecta* 'Erythroblastos'
Halesia diptera
Lagerstroemia indica
Prunus 'Spire'

NARROWLY COLUMNAR
Acer saccharum 'Newton Sentry'
Calocedrus decurrens 'Berrima Gold'
Juniperus chinensis 'Spartan'
Pinus sylvestris 'Fastigiata'
Prunus 'Amanogawa'

BROADLY SPREADING
Albizia julibrissin f. *rosea*
Catalpa bignonioides 'Aurea'
Chionanthus retusus
Prunus × *subhirtella* 'Autumnalis'
Sorbus alnifolia

BROADLY CONICAL
Cornus alternifolia
Ligustrum lucidum
Magnolia salicifolia
Malus tschonoskii
Oxydendrum arboreum

NARROWLY CONICAL
Abies koreana
Betula populifolia
Cupressus arizonica 'Pyramidalis'
Juniperus chinensis 'Aurea'
Pyrus calleryana 'Chanticleer'

WEEPING
Buddleja alternifolia
Caragana arborescens 'Pendula'
Ilex aquifolium 'Argentea Marginata Pendula'
Malus 'Red Jade'
Prunus 'Kiku-shidare-zakura'

SCREENS AND BOUNDARIES

TREES FREQUENTLY NEED to be useful as well as ornamental. One of their prime functions is to screen an area from the sights and sounds of the outside world. Trees are also good for dividing a space, separating a vegetable garden from an ornamental area, for example, or concealing an unsightly structure. In exposed sites, a boundary screen is particularly beneficial since it gives protection, enabling more delicate plants to be grown.

SCREENING WITH TREES

In large properties, a traditional boundary screen consists of a belt of large trees planted around the perimeter of the area; the trees are chosen to blend in well with the surrounding countryside so that they do not appear obtrusive, while more ornamental plantings are usually reserved for areas closer to the house. In smaller areas, however, where space is at a premium, boundary plantings need to be both functional and decorative.

Hedges composed of single species of privet (*Ligustrum*) and cypresses (*Chamaecyparis*, × *Cupressocyparis*, and *Cupressus*) are often used for boundary plantings in small properties. While these are functional, they often lack interest and provide little ornamental appeal. They can also require considerable maintenance, particularly when composed of fast-growing plants such as Leyland cypress (× *Cupressocyparis leylandii*).

As an alternative to the traditional hedge, trees can provide effective, varied, and decorative screens, especially when combined with ornamental shrubs. A single carefully placed specimen can hide an unsightly view, building, or neighbor's window, while a line of mixed trees will quickly seclude an area and provide interest throughout the year.

PRIVATE REFUGE
*Using ornamental trees
makes a screen attractive
as well as useful. Here, a
normally large tree,* Acer
platanoides *'Drummondii',
has been used to enclose part
of a garden, obscuring a
greenhouse to the rear.
Grown so close to each other,
these maples would soon
shade this area, so they need
to be cut back regularly to
restrict their size and keep
them compact.*

◀ A SPLASH OF COLOR
An existing boundary planting of evergreens can be enlivened considerably by planting an occasional deciduous tree in front. The bright autumn color of these maples, Acer capillipes *and A.* palmatum, *is an effective foil to the dark evergreen foliage.*

▼ CREATING A BOUNDARY
A boundary composed of a mixture of ornamental trees and shrubs – deciduous and evergreen – is both functional and attractive. Here, Acer negundo *'Flamingo', a maple with variegated leaves, stands out among the other trees.*

CHOOSING THE RIGHT TREES

For screens and boundary plantings, select trees that are reasonably fast growing, hardy, and will withstand exposure if necessary. To create a dense screen, avoid trees that are very open in habit, such as *Aralia*, and those that are relatively late into leaf, such as *Catalpa*, *Gleditsia*, and *Robinia*, since for much of the year these will be without foliage. Combining

> Trees can conceal eyesores and provide privacy in an area

deciduous and evergreen trees ensures seasonal variety as well as a certain degree of privacy. For additional interest, use trees of various shapes, such as an upright holly (*Ilex*) with a spreading hawthorn (*Crataegus*). A narrow habit is particularly effective and useful where there is limited space, for example when a dividing screen is required in a small area: trees such as hollies and *Pittosporum tenuifolium* are ideal.

SUITABLE TREES

DECIDUOUS
Acer campestre
Acer platanoides 'Globosum'
Carpinus betulus 'Columnaris'
Crataegus laevigata
Malus cultivars

EVERGREEN
Ilex × *altaclerensis/I. aquifolium* cultivars
Laurus nobilis
Ligustrum lucidum cultivars
Photinia × *fraseri* cultivars
Pittosporum tenuifolium

CREATING SHADE AND SHELTER

EXPOSED AND OPEN AREAS in your yard can be inhospitable, since they are often cold and windy in winter and hot and dry in summer. However, with one or two carefully placed trees, you can create a very pleasant shady or sheltered spot. Trees provide ideal conditions for an underplanting of shade-loving shrubs and perennials; they also offer a canopy under which you can sit and relax, protected to a great extent from the elements.

LIGHT AND DENSE SHADE

All trees create shade, but the amount of shade they give varies considerably depending on the kind of tree. Shape is a key factor: spreading trees cast a greater area of shade than conical or columnar ones, for example. The depth of shade, whether it is deep or light and dappled, depends on the density of a tree's foliage. For a woodland-style planting of shade-loving shrubs and perennials, a spreading tree provides the most suitable conditions.

The kinds of plants that can be used beneath a tree will depend on the space available; again, this is greatly influenced by the tree's shape, as well as the height at which it branches. A weeping tree, with branches sweeping to the ground, will give little scope for underplanting, whereas there is space to grow many shrubs and perennials beneath a rounded or spreading

▲ SHADY RETREAT
A mature Magnolia × soulangeana *is highlighted by a functional and ornamental circular bench, making it an inviting place to sit, either beneath the flowers in spring or the dense, leafy shade in summer.*

◀ SHADE-LOVING PLANTING
Tree canopies provide shelter for many shade-loving plants. Here, a 'Victoria' plum tree filters the sun from a planting of woodland perennials, including hostas and corydalis.

tree (*see p.37*). If you wish to grow plants that require light but benefit from shelter, such as rhododendrons, azaleas, camellias, and *Pieris*, two or more trees planted at about one-and-a-half to two times their spread apart will provide suitable conditions. Position the plants toward the edge of the canopy.

For a large area of shade, use spreading rather than conical or columnar trees

There is more flexibility in the type of tree you can choose if the area beneath it is not planted but instead houses a bench or circular seat, for example. An attractive seating arrangement also serves to draw attention to a specimen tree. Established trees may also be used as supports for hammocks or swings in the shade.

TREES TO CREATE SHADE

DAPPLED SHADE
Albizia julibrissin f. *rosea*
Carpinus caroliniana
Gleditsia triacanthos
Koelreuteria paniculata
Prunus × *subhirtella* 'Autumnalis'
Styrax japonicus

DENSE SHADE
Cornus kousa
Crataegus phaenopyrum
Laburnum × *watereri* 'Vossii'
Magnolia × *soulangeana*
Malus (many)
Photinia × *fraseri*
Prunus sargentii

A PLACE FOR REST AND SHELTER
These two crabapples could have shaded a woodland planting, but they are equally valuable for creating a sheltered resting place on a hot, sunny day.

SPECIMEN TREES

WHILE SOME TREES form a functional backdrop, such as those planted on a boundary, others take center stage, placed at strategic points to display their striking ornamental characteristics to best effect. Specimen trees can be used as focal points in their own right or may serve to highlight a particular setting. They may also lead the eye to another area, frame a distant view, or mark the division between two distinct areas.

USING SPECIMEN TREES

There is a diverse range of small trees suitable as feature specimens. Although the kind of tree to plant is, to a large extent, a matter of personal taste, there are several criteria to take into account when making your choice. A specimen tree should have one or more bold characteristics, and it must be sufficiently impressive to stand on its own, either contrasting with or complementing nearby plantings. It must also be of a suitable size for its position; if a tree is too large, or too small, it will not achieve the desired effect.

Many trees planted as specimens are chosen for their flowers, fruit, or foliage, but a strong shape adds greatly to the impact of a tree. For this reason, many weeping trees make ideal features. Trees with a strong, upright habit are also useful, particularly when they have the added bonus of ornamental foliage.

> A specimen tree must have bold characteristics and, preferably, a strong shape

Specimen trees can occupy many positions in an area, provided they are not hidden among other plants. Use them to highlight a particular area or to draw the eye to a far corner. They can also be used effectively to

BOLD BORDER FEATURE
*The extremely pendulous habit and bold purple leaves make the weeping purple beech (*Fagus sylvatica *'Purpurea Pendula') an eye-catching specimen tree. This one has been grafted low down to make a small tree, but these beeches are frequently taller, with branches weeping to the ground and mushroom-shaped heads. A tree this size makes a good specimen only because it is in scale with the surrounding plants in the border; it would be ineffective in a more open position.*

SUITABLE TREES

DECIDUOUS
Acer pseudoplatanus 'Brilliantissimum'
Betula (many)
Catalpa bignonioides 'Aurea'
Cornus controversa
Fagus sylvatica 'Dawyck Gold'
Pyrus calleryana 'Chanticleer'

EVERGREEN
Arbutus × *andrachnoides*
Cupressus arizonica 'Pyramidalis'
Ilex aquifolium/I. × *altaclerensis* cultivars
Ligustrum lucidum 'Excelsum Superbum'
Magnolia virginiana var. *australis*
Photinia × *fraseri*
Picea pungens f. *glauca*
Trachycarpus fortunei

◄STRIKING FOCAL POINT
A weeping silver pear, Pyrus salicifolia *'Pendula', with its lower branches removed, has a prominent position in the center of intersecting paths.*

add ornament to garden structures, such as a flight of steps or a pond. A carefully placed pair of trees can be used to frame an attractive view.

Specimen trees are often placed in the center of a lawn, although this is not always the best position for them. Consider instead planting one at the side, perhaps either next to a patio or terrace, where it can cast its shade, or in or close to an adjacent border, where its strong shape will draw the eye from the expanse of green. In borders or island beds, trees provide a useful contrast to lower-growing perennials and shrubs, such as hostas and dwarf conifers, adding often-needed height.

▲ LAWN SPECIMEN
A tree placed to the side of a lawn often makes more impact than one positioned in the center, as is shown by this Prunus × subhirtella *'Autumnalis'.*

MULTISEASONAL TREES

IN MANY CASES, trees have only one outstanding ornamental feature – flowers, autumn color, or fruits, for example. However, there is a good selection of those that have a number of decorative qualities that span two or more seasons. These trees are known as "multiseasonal," and they are invaluable in small spaces. If you only have space for one or two trees, it is particularly important that they provide interest for most, if not all, of the year.

TREES FOR ALL SEASONS

Flowers are frequently one of the main reasons for choosing a tree. However, a tree that may be striking in bloom for a few weeks can often look relatively dull the rest of the year. When choosing a tree for multi-seasonal interest, other ornamental features must be taken into account, such as fruit, foliage, bark and stems, and habit.

Trees with eye-catching flowers as well as ornamental fruits include the crabapples (*Malus*) and mountain ashes (*Sorbus*). Those with flowers and good autumn color include the cherries *Prunus* 'Okame' and *P. sargentii*. Some trees, such as many *Malus* and *Photinia villosa*, have attractive flowers and fruit and good autumn color.

Interesting bark is a very important aspect of many multiseasonal trees, since it will be an attraction throughout the year. Combine ornamental bark with other features, such as flowers in *Stewartia pseudocamellia*, which also has good autumn color. Some trees have specific winter features that add to their value, extending the season of

▶ SPRING FLOWERS
Amelanchier lamarckii *starts its show with profuse white flowers in mid-spring, accompanied by attractive young foliage, bronze with silky hairs.*

▲ AUTUMN COLOR
After the long display of flowers, purple-black fruits, and spring and summer foliage, Amelanchier lamarckii *exhibits its magnificent bright autumn colors.*

interest. The maple *Acer pensylvanicum* 'Erythrocladum', for example, has brilliant pink winter shoots combined with yellow-streaked bark, as well as yellow autumn leaves. Evergreens are invaluable in the multiseasonal garden, but they should not

Multiseasonal trees must have two or preferably more seasons of interest

be used exclusively, since their foliage shows less variation than deciduous trees. However, some evergreens are multiseasonal trees in their own right. Interesting *Arbutus* × *andrachnoides* has attractive bark as well as flowers and fruit, while many hollies (*Ilex*) are useful for their often variegated leaves and their colorful fruits.

▲ CRABAPPLE IN AUTUMN
Many of the crabapples are attractive over more than one season. Malus 'Golden Hornet' is best known for its autumn fruits, but it also bears white flowers from pink buds in spring.

◄ CHERRY IN WINTER
Trees grown primarily for their bark, such as Prunus serrula, are a particularly welcome sight in winter. This cherry also has bowl-shaped white flowers in spring, followed by cherrylike fruits and yellow autumn leaves.

MULTISEASONAL TREES

Acer (many, *see p.62*)
Amelanchier
Cornus (many)
Cotoneaster 'Hybridus Pendulus'
Crataegus crus-galli, C. viridis 'Winter King'
Franklinia alatamaha
Malus (many)
Photinia × *fraseri*
Prunus 'Okame'
Pyrus calleryana 'Chanticleer'
Sorbus
Viburnum sieboldii

TREES FOR FLOWERS OR FRUITS

MOST TREES PRODUCE FLOWERS, and while these are sometimes insignificant, many trees are grown specifically for their spectacular, occasionally fragrant, blooms. Flowers provide a relatively brief display; if you have space for only a few trees, choose those that also produce attractive fruits to prolong the season of interest. In a small space, where trees are viewed at close quarters, even tiny flowers can be highly ornamental, such as those of maples (*Acer*), the hanging catkins of birches (*Betula*), or the dark, honey-scented flowers of *Pittosporum*.

EARLY OFFERINGS

Most trees produce their flowers in spring, including some of the most popular flowering trees, such as the cherries (*Prunus*). These range from the early flowering forms of the cherry plums (*P. cerasifera*) to the Japanese cherries, some of which, such as *P.* 'Shirofugen', flower late in the season. Spring is also

Trees with striking fruits as well as flowers are ideal for small spaces

the flowering time for most of the crab-apples (*Malus*), many of which have the additional bonus of ornamental fruits.

Magnolias also offer excellent flowers in spring. *M.* × *soulangeana* is a popular choice, but more unusual are the forms of *M.* × *loebneri*, such as 'Leonard Messel', with starry pink flowers. There are also the summer-flowering magnolias, including *M. tripetala*, with headily fragrant flowers and large red fruit clusters in autumn.

The flowering dogwoods (*Cornus*) have tiny, insignificant flowers, but very showy bracts surrounding them. Among the most spectacular of these are *C.* × *rutgersensis* series, including 'Stellar Pink' and 'Aurora', which are hybrids of *C. florida* and *C. kousa*. They bloom between the parents' bloom times and have superior disease resistance.

FRUIT CLUSTERS IN AUTUMN
This hawthorn, Crataegus persimilis *'Prunifolia', bears attractive white flowers in late spring. Another great season of interest is autumn, when the clusters of bright red fruits combine with the coloring foliage to produce a stunning display.*

▲ SPRING SPLENDOR
*The large, showy white
flowers of* Magnolia
salicifolia *'Wada's Memory'
cover the tree in spring.*

◄ GOLDEN SHOWER
*In spring, the pendulous
yellow flower clusters of*
Laburnum × watereri *'Vossii'
make a spectacular sight.*

LATE ATTRACTIONS

As summer progresses, the number of trees
flowering becomes fewer, but there are still
some that are at their best at this time.
Lagerstroemia indica and *Stewartia ovata*
are examples of fine flowering trees for late
summer, while *Albizia julibrissin* and
Koelreuteria paniculata take the display
toward autumn, the latter developing
ornamental pods after the yellow flowers
fade. The white flowers of *Aralia elata* are
often produced as the leaves color.
Numerous fruiting trees are at their best
in autumn, such as the wide variety of
crabapples, and Korean mountain ash
(*Sorbus alnifolia*). Some flowers are
produced even in winter, namely those
of the strawberry trees (*Arbutus*), which
bear their red fruits at the same time,
and *Prunus* × *subhirtella*, which blooms
from autumn to spring in mild areas.

RECOMMENDED TREES

TREES FOR FLOWERS

Cornus (flowering dogwoods, *see p.65*)
Halesia monticola
Koelreuteria paniculata
Laburnum × *watereri* 'Vossii'
Magnolia (many)
Malus (many)
Prunus (many)
Stewartia pseudocamellia

TREES FOR FRUITS

Abies koreana
Cornus florida, C. kousa
Crataegus (several; not double forms)
Ilex (many)
Koelreuteria paniculata
Malus (many)
Sorbus (many)
Viburnum sieboldii

TREES FOR FOLIAGE

F LOWERS AND FRUITS are frequently a tree's most striking assets, yet they provide interest for only a few weeks. Foliage, however, is a much longer-lasting feature, which should always be a prime consideration when choosing a tree. Leaves offer an immense diversity of sizes, shapes, colors, and textures. If you have space for several trees, combine a variety of leaf types, both deciduous and evergreen, to create attractive, contrasting effects.

DECIDUOUS TREES

Trees with variegated or colored leaves are often very attractive, especially when contrasted with green foliage. However, they should be used sparingly, particularly in a small space, where too many of them may overwhelm other plants. For seasonal variety, use trees that have variously colored foliage in spring or autumn but are green-leaved much of the time in between, such as *Acer pseudoplatanus*

'Brilliantissimum', which has excellent early pink leaves. Many trees are grown for their attractively shaped leaves. The maples (*Acer*), for example, have very ornamental leaves, which develop good autumn color, while *Alnus glutinosa* 'Imperialis' combines deeply cut foliage with a graceful habit. Trees with large, bold leaves are also effective, such as those of the fig tree (*Ficus carica*) or *Aralia elata*, which may color attractively in autumn.

▲ PINKISH HUES
The striking pinkish spring foliage of Aesculus × neglecta *'Erythroblastos' offers an outstanding but rather short-lived display of color.*

▶ LEAFY CONTRAST
Picea pungens f. glauca *provides a good evergreen backdrop for the climbing golden-leaved hops,* Humulus lupulus *'Aureus'.*

▲ FRESH GREEN MAPLE
Maples, like this Acer
shirasawanum *'Aureum',
shown here in late spring,
provide colorful foliage as
well as interesting leaf shapes.*

◄ SEASONAL CHANGES
*Autumn is one of the most
spectacular times for foliage
color, with many maples, such
as this* Acer triflorum, *turning
to shades of red.*

EVERGREEN TREES

Evergreens generally show less variation in
their foliage throughout the year than
deciduous trees (exceptions to this include
Pinus sylvestris 'Aurea', with bright yellow
foliage in winter). However, evergreen trees
have the advantage of providing winter
foliage that can often be used as an
effective background for other plants.
The upright forms of yew (*Taxus*) for
example, have dark green foliage that is
an ideal foil to lighter-leaved deciduous
trees, such as the yellow-leaved maple,
Acer shirasawanum 'Aureum'. Many
evergreens are also excellent foliage plants
in their own right. The variegated hollies,
which include forms of *Ilex* × *altaclerensis*
and *I. aquifolium*, provide both attractive
foliage and fruits, while the yellow-leaved
form of bay laurel (*Laurus nobilis* 'Aurea')
has colorful, aromatic foliage.

FOLIAGE TREES

DECIDUOUS
Acer (many)
Catalpa bignonioides 'Aurea'
Cornus controversa 'Variegata'
Crataegus
Fagus sylvatica cultivars
Magnolia virginiana
Prunus sargentii
Sorbus (mountain ashes)

EVERGREEN
Ilex (many)
Illicium anisatum
Juniperus chinensis 'Aurea'
Laurus nobilis 'Aurea'
Photinia × *fraseri*
Pinus sylvestris 'Aurea'
Pittosporum tenuifolium and cultivars
Taxus baccata cultivars

TREES FOR BARK OR SHOOTS

THE ORNAMENTAL QUALITIES of bark and shoots are often overlooked, yet they are among the few features that can be appreciated throughout the year. Tree bark may be beautifully colored or patterned, or intriguing in texture, and planting just one of the many trees grown for this effect will add greatly to the interest of an area. Attractive bark is particularly valuable as a winter feature, combining well with trees grown for their ornamental shoots.

ATTRACTIONS OF BARK

The bark of a tree changes with age: as the trunk grows taller and thickens, the outer bark must expand to accommodate it. In some trees, the bark splits into ridges, often very deep; in others, the bark peels off in strips or patches, and falls as new bark is produced to replace it. Both of these methods of renewal can produce striking effects, particularly evident in the streaked stems of the snakebark maples, the flaking bark of *Lagerstroemia* and *Stewartia*, and the peeling trunks of birches (*Betula*) and *Prunus serrula*. Some barks have other ornamental qualities, such as the prominently spiny stems of *Aralia elata*, or the fibrous trunk of *Trachycarpus fortunei*. Trees that are grown for their bark are best planted in an open position, so that their attractive trunks are not obscured by surrounding plants. Close to a path is ideal, since the tactile as well as visual qualities of bark may be enjoyed. Birches make good focal points, since their clean white stems stand out well, even at a distance, either planted on their own or with a suitable contrasting background.

Bark may be washed with a damp cloth (to remove green algae) and touched gently without causing harm, but never peel off strips from birches or cherries, since this will damage the delicate tissues beneath.

▼ PAPERBARK MAPLE
The attractive peeling, cinnamon-colored bark on its trunk and branches places Acer griseum *among the most sought-after trees grown for this feature.*

Vivid winter shoots

◀ BRIGHT SHOOTS
The young shoots of Acer palmatum *'Senkaki' turn deep pink in winter.*

◀ STRIPED MAPLE
Attractive green- and
white-streaked bark is
one of the many
subtle qualities of the
snakebark maples,
shown here in Acer
pensylvanicum.

▲ HIMALAYAN BIRCH
Betula utilis var.
jacquemontii is one of
the most eye-catching
trees grown for bark,
especially when set
against a darker
background.

TREES WITH STRIKING SHOOTS

Trees grown for their ornamental shoots
usually show this feature best in winter.
Maples (Acer) and willows (Salix)
predominate. Those used are generally
small trees, such as Acer palmatum
'Senkaki'. Any large trees are usually
coppiced or pollarded to promote vigorous
young shoots for winter color and to
restrict the tree's size in order to keep the
shoots closer to eye level (see p.57).

GOOD CHOICES

TREES FOR ORNAMENTAL BARK

Acer (A. griseum and all snakebark maples,
see p.62)
Arbutus × andrachnoides
Betula
Lagerstroemia
Pinus bungeana
Prunus maackii and P. serrula
Pseudocydonia sinensis
Stewartia pseudocamellia

TREES FOR COLORFUL SHOOTS

Acer pensylvanicum 'Erythrocladum'
Salix alba 'Britzensis' and subsp. vitellina
Salix 'Erythroflexuosa'

TREES TO ATTRACT WILDLIFE

ALL TREES ATTRACT AND ENCOURAGE some sort of wildlife: birds roost and nest in their branches and eat their berries, and insects pollinate the flowers (unless they are wind pollinated). Many insects also find a home on the tree or in the soil or detritus beneath, attracting birds who feed on them. Many birds are invaluable for controlling garden pests such as caterpillars, slugs, and aphids, provided chemical controls are not used.

ENCOURAGING WILDLIFE

Some trees have features that are particularly attractive to wildlife. Densely leaved trees, such as the evergreen conifers *Chamaecyparis*, *Cupressus*, and *Thuja*, provide ideal shelter and cover for birds, especially during winter. Hawthorns (*Crataegus*) are also good, in particular the forms of *C. phaenopyrum*.

ATTRACTION FOR BEES
The eye-catching, tubular red flowers of Aesculus pavia *attract a variety of bees and other insects in late spring and early summer.*

There is usually plenty of food available for nectar-feeding insects, such as pollinating bees, butterflies, or moths, at the peak of the flowering season. For most trees, this is in mid- to late spring, so it is useful to include some trees that flower either earlier or later. *Amelanchier*, for example, flowers early in the year; it also produces fruits early, providing food for birds in summer, when berries are otherwise scarce. Late-flowering trees that are good for wildlife include *Lagerstroemia indica* and *Stewartia pseudocamellia*. Both flower in summer.

> ### Encourage songbirds into your yard: they will help keep many pests at bay

Any of the berrying trees are a valuable source of food in autumn and winter, with hawthorns, hollies, crabapples, and mountain ashes (*Sorbus*) among the best. If you are choosing a tree with the purpose of attracting wildlife, avoid those with double flowers, since they do not produce fruit. Hollies (*Ilex*) are excellent, since their fruits are persistent, providing food well into winter. Yellow fruits are less attractive to birds, so choose trees with red fruits.

To attract a wider range of wildlife, consider developing "wild" or moist areas, such as a pond or boggy area, within the garden. Plant shrubs and perennials, as well as trees, to provide food and shelter and to encourage birds and other animals.

◄ FEAST FOR BIRDS
*The striking orange-
red fruits of the
mountain ash* (Sorbus
aucuparia) *are very
attractive to birds
when they ripen,
providing welcome
food in autumn.*

▼ REFUGE FOR BIRDS
*Fruits tempt birds to
feed in a garden in
autumn, while a
carefully positioned
nesting box may
encourage them to
become at least
temporary residents.*

FAVORITES FOR WILDLIFE

Aesculus (bees, butterflies, and birds)
Amelanchier (bees, butterflies, and birds)
Chamaecyparis (roosting sites for birds)
Crataegus (bees, butterflies, and birds)
Cupressus (roosting sites for birds)
Ilex (bees, butterflies, and birds)
Malus (bees, butterflies, and birds)
Sorbus (bees, butterflies, and birds)
Stewartia (bees, butterflies, and birds)
Thuja (roosting sites for birds)
Viburnum (bees, butterflies, and birds)

CONTAINER TREES

CONTAINERS BRING A GREAT degree of flexibility to planting and are ideal for small spaces where planting space may be limited or even nonexistent, such as on a roof or in a courtyard. A great advantage of containers is that they are easy to move around, enabling ever-changing displays. They also allow you to grow trees that have specific needs, such as tender trees, which can be moved to a protected place for winter, or trees that require an acidic soil.

CHOOSING AND PLACING TREES

Many trees are suitable for growing in containers. The best are those that are naturally small or slow-growing, or ones that may be pruned regularly. Large, fast-growing trees, such as birches (*Betula*), soon outgrow their containers and may become top-heavy and subject to blowing over in strong winds.

For long-term display, choose an evergreen such as a *Chamaecyparis* or *Photinia* × *fraseri*, or a deciduous tree grown for its foliage, such as *Acer palmatum*, particularly the cut-leaved forms. If there is space for a variety of trees, you could consider those with effects over a shorter period, such as flowering trees, including *Hydrangea paniculata* and *Caragana arborescens* trained as standards, or some of the flowering cherries: *Prunus* 'Amanogawa' would be a good choice.

Trees in containers associate well with formal plantings and are particularly suited to areas close to the house. They are useful

For roof gardens, choose lightweight containers, such as plastic or wood

for extending gardening onto paved areas, for example a patio, or may be used to highlight certain areas or structures, such as a gateway, flight of steps, or a door. Potted trees combine well with other container-grown plants, including shrubs, perennials, and annuals, to provide an exciting range of effects. For variety (and providing they are not too

GROUPING CONTAINERS

Container trees have real impact when combined with other plants, their height adding interest to any display. Here, the silvery foliage of Elaeagnus angustifolia *contrasts with a range of colorful perennials.*

TREES FOR POTS

SUNNY SITES
Caragana arborescens
'Pendula'
Chamaecyparis obtusa
Eriobotrya japonica
Ficus carica
Hydrangea paniculata
Lagerstroemia
Laurus nobilis
Ligustrum lucidum
Pinus sylvestris 'Fastigiata'
Prunus 'Amanogawa',
P. 'Kiku-shidare-zakura'

SHADY SITES
Acer palmatum
Ilex
Laurus nobilis
Ligustrum lucidum
Photinia × *fraseri*
Pittosporum tenuifolium
Taxus baccata 'Fastigiata'
and 'Standishii'

EVERGREEN DISPLAY
Placed in a prominent position and pruned to retain a compact shape (see p.56), Ilex × altaclerensis *'Golden King' makes an attractive year-round feature.*

heavy), move the containers around to create changing combinations of flowering or foliage plants. Place container trees that flower or fruit briefly but profusely in a prominent location when they are at their best, to make the most of their assets. After the period of interest is over, move them to another, less conspicuous position in the yard, perhaps in a border.

CHOOSING CONTAINERS
There is a wide range of different pots available, made from a variety of materials including wood, stone, terracotta, plastic, and fiberglass. Stone and terracotta pots are attractive but relatively heavy, so if weight is a consideration, for example on a rooftop, choose lightweight containers, such as those made of plastic, fiberglass, or wood. Since trees are long-lived, it is important to select a container that will last. While wooden or plastic containers are relatively inexpensive, they tend to rot or split. Unless the garden is very mild, choose a pot that is frostproof, since some containers (particularly terracotta) are damaged during cold weather.

Always consider which size, color, and shape of pot will suit the tree as well as the style and scale of the area. A container should add to, rather than detract from, the area in which it is placed.

PATIO FEATURE
*The many forms
of* Acer palmatum
*make delightful
foliage plants and
adapt extremely well
to containers. They
require a sheltered
site, preferably with
some shade from very
hot sun, and may
need some protection
from late frosts.*

CITY GARDENS

Gardens in urban areas may be very small, often mostly paved, and with little area for planting. They are therefore ideal sites for using trees in containers. Such spaces are also likely to be subject to special climatic conditions. They may well be relatively mild and sheltered from wind and can be very shady but with some parts exposed to periods of hot sun. Trees therefore need to be chosen accordingly. If conditions are particularly mild, a city garden can provide the opportunity to experiment with some trees normally grown in subtropical areas, such as citrus fruits or palms.

In a very small space, choose mainly evergreen trees, or deciduous ones with attractive foliage to ensure a long season of interest. Aim to keep the size of the tree to scale with the garden. Container trees will form only part of the ornamental attractions, so allow sufficient space for other pots of flowering shrubs, perennials, and annuals to create a display that is effective all year. In cities, where the air may be polluted, select trees that will tolerate these conditions, such as bay laurel (*Laurus nobilis*) and yews (*Taxus*). For exposed, windy rooftops, avoid top-heavy trees, such as *Aralia elata*.

URBAN TREES

Acer japonicum, A. palmatum
Crataegus viridis 'Winter King'
Cupressus sempervirens
Eriobotrya japonica
Gleditsia triacanthos
Ilex × *altaclerensis, I. aquifolium*
Koelreuteria paniculata
Lagerstroemia indica
Ligustrum lucidum 'Excelsum Superbum'
Ostrya virginiana
Photinia × *fraseri*
Prunus sargentii

CARING FOR TREES IN POTS

Trees grown in containers need more careful maintenance than those planted in the open ground. Since the small quantity of soil mix in a pot can hold only limited amounts of water and nutrients, trees in containers can dry out easily and will eventually become depleted of nutrients. At planting, use a good, soil based mix with an added slow-release fertilizer. During hot weather, you may need to water twice a day (if the tree needs acidic soil and your water is hard, use only rainwater collected in a barrel). The soil mix should always remain slightly moist. To prevent drying out, apply bark chips, cocoa shells, or pebbles to the surface. Waterlogging is also often a problem for container plants, so make sure you have provided for adequate drainage before planting.

Every year, in spring, remove the mulch and the top 2in (5cm) of soil mix, then replace it with fresh mix with added fertilizer. Every three to five years, again in spring, repot the tree into either the same or a larger container. To repot, remove the

> ## Container trees need frequent watering and repotting every few years

tree from its container, tease out the roots, and remove some of the old soil mix, cutting back any large, thick roots by up to one-third. Soak the root ball if necessary, then repot the tree using fresh mix and mulch. Prune container trees in the same way as you would trees grown in the open ground (*see pp.50–53*).

◄ CITY GARDEN
An array of container plants, including the evergreen trees Cordyline australis *and* Pittosporum tenuifolium, *create an attractive display in this courtyard.*

▼ BLUE SPRUCE
Conifers like this Picea pungens f. glauca *are good container trees, since their roots do not require much space.*

Trees with Other Plants

WHILE TREES CAN LOOK SPLENDID in an isolated position, for example when planted at the end of a vista, they can also be grown very effectively with other plants, including bulbs, herbaceous perennials, shrubs, and climbers. Depending on the look you wish to achieve, you can either combine plants that flower or fruit at the same time as the tree, in contrasting or complementary colors, or extend the season by providing interest at other times of the year.

Which Kind of Tree?

When growing trees in combination with other plants, one of the main points to consider is the amount of shade that the tree produces, since this will determine which plants may be grown beneath. Birches, for example, cast relatively little shade, but they are hungry feeders and quickly remove water and nutrients from the soil. Barberries (*Berberis*), dogwoods (*Cornus*), and many *Euonymus* are therefore ideal planting companions, since they thrive in a light position and a poor soil. Beneath trees that create denser shade, for example many spreading or weeping trees, you will need to choose plants that require little light.

Bulbous plants that produce their flowers and foliage before the tree's leaves are fully open are excellent under trees.

The shape and size of the tree are also important factors. A strongly pendulous tree with branches weeping to the ground will hide anything planted beneath it, except perhaps for some early-flowering bulbs. An upright tree, however, will be able to accommodate a broader selection of plants at its base.

LIGHT, AIRY CANOPY
The light shade cast by Betula utilis *var.* jacquemontii *allows a wide range of plants to grow beneath, providing an ample foil to its handsome white bark.*

▲ SPRING DISPLAY
Prunus pendula *creates dense shade in summer, but the grape hyacinths and primroses bloom before the leaves are fully open.*

▶ USEFUL PARTNERS
Clematis alpina *is an ideal climber for a small tree. Plant it at the canopy edge and train it using a stake.*

SHADE-LOVING PLANTS TO GROW WITH TREES

BULBS
Anemone
Cyclamen
Eranthis
Galanthus
Hyacinthoides
Erythronium
Scilla
Trillium

CLIMBERS
Actinidia kolomikta
Clematis (some)
Eccremocarpus scaber
Humulus lupulus 'Aureus'
Lathyrus latifolius
Lonicera
Parthenocissus
Rosa

PERENNIALS
Anemone (Japanese anemones)
Astilbe
Astrantia
Bergenia
Digitalis
Epimedium
Euphorbia amygdaloides subsp. *robbiae*
Hosta

SHRUBS
Aucuba japonica
Daphne
Eleutherococcus
Euonymus (evergreen sorts)
Mahonia
Pieris
Skimmia
Viburnum

▲ SHRUBBY MIX
A young maple, Acer
palmatum *'Senkaki',
combines with shrubs
including* Sorbaria aitchisonii
and Rosa nitida *in an island
bed to create a blend of
texture and color.*

▶ NATURAL SETTING
*Areas intended to have a
natural appearance, such as a
wildflower planting, are best
complemented by trees that
blend in well with the
landscape, for example this*
Crataegus laciniata.

USING TREES WITH OTHER PLANTS

If a tree is intended as a specimen, then avoid underplanting with large shrubs, since they will mask the trunk and shape of the tree. Instead, choose low, spreading plants, such as periwinkles (*Vinca*) or creeping junipers (*Juniperus horizontalis*), both of which will accentuate a tree's form. However, if the tree is used for screening, you could use larger plants, such as *Prunus laurocerasus* and many *Viburnum*, which will help to fill in the screen.

> Many early-flowering
> bulbs grow happily
> under densely shady trees

Trees also add substance to mixed borders. When selecting plants to associate with trees, consider which ones are in flower when the tree is at its best for maximum impact. Alternatively, use other plants to provide interest over a long period and to enliven the border when the tree is not in its prime. Where a few small trees are grown together, the area can soon begin to take on a "woodland" feel, particularly if underplanted with herbaceous perennials such as astrantias, epimediums, and hostas.

Trees are the perfect hosts for many climbing plants: the trunk and branches provide essential support, while the climber adorns the tree with its additional crop of flowers. The climber must be compatible with the tree. For small ornamental trees, avoid very vigorous climbers, such as wisteria and *Clematis montana*, and instead use slower-growing species such as *C. alpina* and *C. macropetala*.

Ivies are commonly grown as groundcover under trees, and most will grow well in shade. For best effect, use the more vigorous ones, such as *Hedera colchica* 'Dentata Variegata' and *H. hibernica*, in the shadiest places. Climbing ivies may eventually smother a small, ornamental tree, so cut them back before they become a problem. Allow ivies to establish and climb naturally if desired, rather than training them with a support.

LAWN HIGHLIGHTS
Trees are best planted slightly to the side of a lawn, not in the center. Removing the lower branches makes the grass easier to cut and maintain (see pp.52–53, 55).

TREES FOR LAWNS

Acer griseum
Catalpa bignoniodes **'Aurea'**
Cercis canadensis
Chionanthus virginicus
Fagus sylvatica **'Dawyck Gold'**
Koelreuteria paniculata
Magnolia obovata
Malus (many)
Prunus (many)
Sorbus (many)

Planting and Tree Care

Selecting a Tree

Any garden tree is a long-term investment, so it is worth taking some time to decide which tree to plant and where, and to select a good and healthy specimen. This could mean the difference between a plant that grows quickly, or one that produces little or no growth. If possible, buy the tree from the garden center or nursery where it has been grown. Always check that any tree you choose is suited to the conditions that your garden provides.

Establishing your Trees

Once you have selected a suitable tree for the site, it is vital to give it proper attention before, during, and after planting. Prepare the planting hole thoroughly, and always plant the tree at the correct height (never too deeply), since it may sink even lower as the soil settles. After planting, water well, and then frequently for the first year. Check tree ties regularly: overly tight ties can damage and eventually kill a tree. Also, look out for any signs of pests and diseases (*see pp.58–59*) and animal damage (*see p.48*). Any vegetation around the tree's base will compete for water and nutrients, so keep the area free of weeds and grass.

TIPS FOR SUCCESS
• Ensure that the ultimate size of your chosen tree is suitable for the position in which you wish to plant it.
• Select a healthy, well-shaped specimen.
• Never allow the tree roots to dry out, either before or after planting.
• Check for signs of pests and diseases, and remedy promptly.

ORNAMENTAL BARK
When choosing a tree for bark, such as these Prunus serrula, *examine them before buying to ensure they have clean, undamaged stems.*

◄ ADAPTABLE CHOICE Acer pseudoplatanus *'Brilliantissimum' thrives in sun or partial shade.*

ASSESSING THE SOIL

A HEALTHY SOIL IS VITAL for trees to thrive. The ideal soil contains a well-balanced mixture of clay and sand: it will drain freely but retain moisture, and it is high in nutrients. Too much clay can result in a heavy soil that may become waterlogged when wet. A sandy soil may be impoverished and dry out fast. The type of garden soil you have – whether it is acidic or alkaline or has a high clay or sand content – will determine which trees you can best grow, so it is essential to assess it thoroughly before you decide which tree to plant.

TESTING YOUR SOIL pH

Most trees thrive in a slightly acidic soil, but some do not tolerate alkalinity, particularly if the soil is dry and shallow. The effects of lime include yellowing leaves, little growth, and poor autumn color. The pH of a soil – its level of acidity or alkalinity – is alterable to some extent but not usually successfully for trees, owing to their wide-spreading roots. If you have alkaline soil, it is best not to grow acid-loving trees, such as *Oxydendrum* and some magnolias. Instead, choose those that tolerate lime, such as flowering cherries.

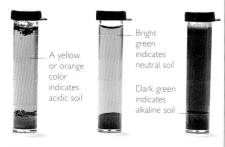

A yellow or orange color indicates acidic soil

Bright green indicates neutral soil

Dark green indicates alkaline soil

USING A SOIL-TEST KIT
Do-it-yourself kits are an effective way to measure your soil pH. For the result, simply match the color in the tube against a chart.

SOIL TEXTURE

The best garden soil is a loam with a good, crumbly texture, not too sticky or gritty when moist, and with ample organic matter. A good soil retains moisture so that it does not dry out easily and drains freely so that it does not become waterlogged. Soils that have a high clay content tend to be fertile but poorly drained and heavy; sandy soils are easier to work but are low in nutrients and subject to drying out; silty soils become easily compacted.

Moist and heavy; can be squeezed into shape

CLAY SOIL
Highly moisture-retentive, a clay soil is sticky and smooth.

Dry and gritty in texture

SANDY SOIL
A sandy soil drains very freely and tends to be light and dry.

SOIL TIPS

• Nearby gardens usually provide a good guide to a soil's pH. If rhododendrons and camellias thrive, then your soil is almost certainly acidic.

• Test more than one area of the garden. Some areas, such as at the foot of a wall, may be more alkaline than others.

• Several trees are suited to heavy clay soils, such as some maples (*Acer negundo*, *A. pseudoplatanus*), horse chestnuts (*Aesculus*), hawthorns (*Crataegus*), and hollies (*Ilex*).

• Trees that grow well on light, sandy soils include birches (*Betula*), *Caragana*, *Cercis*, *Koelreuteria*, and *Robinia*.

IMPROVING THE SOIL

You can improve the texture, drainage, moisture retention, and fertility of soil considerably by digging in a soil improver. If you have clay soil, coarse horticultural sand combined with organic matter or lime will increase aeration and drainage. For sandy soils, add organic matter and small amounts of clay, which will increase water retention and essential nutrients. Silty soils benefit from adding organic matter and a small amount of clay or lime to improve the structure and prevent compaction.

Manure supplies organic matter and nutrients

Coarse sand improves drainage of heavy soils

Bark chips improve water retention and add nutrients

Leafmold encourages earthworms and adds nutrients

SOIL IMPROVERS

• Composted manure (especially horse manure) and leafmold add nutrients to the soil, increase water retention, and encourage earthworms, which aerate the soil.

• Coarse sand will improve drainage in clay soils (always use horticultural sand, never builder's materials). Large amounts may be needed if the soil is very heavy.

• Small amounts of clay added to a sandy or silty soil will improve the soil structure, increase water retention, and add nutrients.

• Lime is useful for improving the structure of heavy or compacted soils. Never use lime at the same time as manure, and avoid it if you grow trees that require an acidic soil.

• Mulches such as leafmold and bark chips keep moisture in the soil, reduce weeds, and protect roots in winter. Apply them to the soil surface, but do not dig them in.

PREPARING THE SOIL FOR PLANTING

Before undertaking any planting, it is essential to prepare the site thoroughly. If planting in spring, begin preparations in autumn, especially in heavy soils, since any large lumps will be broken down by winter action. Remove perennial weeds, especially the more vigorous ones such as quack grass, thistles, and bindweed. If the area is overgrown, cut down the vegetation first, then dig out the roots. Even with the most rigorous methods of cultivation, some small pieces of root will remain. Remove them as the plants appear, before they can become established. Alternatively, use a systemic herbicide, which moves within the plant from the leaves to the roots. Once the area is cleared of weeds, dig in plenty of organic matter.

DIGGING IN
To improve moisture retention and increase the nutrient content of the soil, dig in ample quantities of organic matter, such as leafmold, manure, or well-rotted compost.

BUYING TREES

A WIDE RANGE OF POPULAR trees is usually available at garden centers; however, if you are looking for something a little more unusual, you may need to visit a specialized nursery. Alternatively, consider buying through the mail. Trees are sold bare-root, balled-and-burlapped (B&B), or in containers, depending on the type of tree and time of year. All trees, particularly bare-root and B&B trees, are best planted as soon as possible after purchasing.

WHAT TO LOOK FOR

Before buying a tree, make sure it is suitable for the site and is a healthy, well-shaped specimen. Inspect the shoots and, if the tree is in foliage, the leaves, since both indicate the health of the plant. The trunk must be straight and intact, and the crown should be appropriately filled out for the age and kind of tree.

CRATAEGUS LAEVIGATA
'PAUL'S SCARLET'

CRATAEGUS LAEVIGATA
'PAUL'S SCARLET'
• **Season of interest:** Late spring to early summer.
• **Height:** 25ft (8m)
• **Spread:** 25ft (8m)
• **Hardiness:** Zones 5-8
• **Soil type:** Any that is not waterlogged. Suitable for clay and alkaline soil.
• **Exposure:** Sun or partial shade. Suitable for windy positions.

BUYING HINTS
• Not only are small trees less expensive than larger ones, they are also easier to plant, quicker to establish, and require less aftercare.
• Check that the eventual size of the tree will not be too large for the site.
• Buy stakes and ties when you purchase your tree.

◄ CHECK THE PLANT LABEL
The label gives vital details of the tree's appearance, size after five or ten years, and cultivation requirements.

BARE-ROOT TREES

Trees that are sold bare-root are usually deciduous and are available only during the dormant season (autumn and early spring). They are grown in the open ground and lifted with little or no soil, so the root system is very susceptible to drying out. Check that the roots are healthy, evenly spread, and have not dried out. Leave the wrapping on for protection until the tree is planted. If you cannot plant the tree right away, keep the roots moist and protected from drying out by heeling the tree in (*see Planting Tips, p.47*).

Evenly spreading roots

Coiled, congested roots

GOOD EXAMPLE
Well-developed roots that are spread in all directions are the sign of a healthy tree.

POOR EXAMPLE
Avoid trees with congested or coiled roots: they will rarely establish successfully.

BALLED-AND-BURLAPPED (B&B) TREES

As with bare-root trees, these trees are grown in the open ground but are lifted with a ball of soil around their roots. Burlap or similar wrapping holds the root ball together and prevents drying out. Both deciduous and evergreen trees may be sold this way. The advantages of a B&B tree are that there is less damage to the root system and it is likely to retain moisture better than a bare-root tree. Like bare-root trees, balled-and-burlapped trees are normally available only in autumn and early spring. Before buying, check that the root ball is firm, intact, and has not dried out. If the tree cannot be planted immediately, keep the root ball moist by watering, and, if the tree is evergreen, protect it from drying winds.

HEALTHY
B&B TREE
Many evergreen trees, particularly conifers, are often available as balled-and-burlapped specimens.

Top growth should appear healthy

The root ball should be firm and the burlap intact

CONTAINER-GROWN TREES

Available for much of the year, container-grown trees are evergreen or deciduous and may be planted nearly any time. Before buying, gently remove the tree from its container, if possible, and inspect the root system. If you see a mass of roots circling the pot, or emerging from its base, then the tree is potbound and best avoided. Keep the soil mix moist and the tree in a sheltered site until planting.

◀ GOOD EXAMPLE
This is a healthy container-grown tree with the best chance of survival: some roots are visible and the root ball is firm.

▼ POOR EXAMPLE
The dense mass of congested roots and liverworts on the surface of the soil mix indicate a potbound tree that is unlikely to establish well.

Root ball is often small in relation to top growth

Evenly spaced branch framework

Mesh may restrict growth

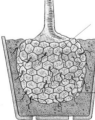

TREE ROOTS IN MESH
Some mature trees are sold with their roots in mesh within a container. Cut the mesh and soak the root ball before planting.

Liverworts on surface of soil mix

Soil mix free of liverworts, weeds, and algae

Healthy, well-developed roots

Potbound root system

Planting a Tree

Careful attention to site preparation and planting greatly increases a tree's ability to establish and grow strongly, rendering it more resistant to disease. Adding well-rotted organic matter will give the tree an excellent start. If planting in spring, add about 4oz (110g) of slow-release fertilizer. For the first two or three years after planting, provide plenty of water, keep the area below the tree weed free, and feed and mulch regularly, not allowing the mulch to touch the trunk. It is easier to plant the tree with a helper to hold it vertical.

How to Plant a Container-grown Tree

The soil mix in a container can dry out very quickly, particularly in warm weather and when a tree is in leaf. Once dry, it can be very difficult to wet again after planting. To prevent a tree from drying out, place the container in water for 30 minutes before planting. Take the tree out of the container just before you are ready to plant.

1 **Mark out** a circular hole, 3–4 times the diameter of the pot. Remove any turf and weeds from the surface, and dig the hole to 1½ times the depth of the pot.

2 **Using a fork**, break up the soil at the sides and base of the hole to enable roots to penetrate more easily. Mix any removed soil with well-rotted organic matter.

3 **Lay the tree** on its side and carefully slide it out of the container. Gently tease out the outer roots without damaging the root ball. This will help the tree establish.

4 **Insert the stake firmly**, slightly off-center, toward the direction of the wind. Add about one-fifth of the mixed soil and organic matter to the hole. Place the tree. Use a stake to check that the top of the root ball is level with the soil.

5 **Backfill with** the soil and organic matter, firming evenly by treading very gently. Tie the tree to the stake. Water and mulch. Cut back any damaged shoots.

HOW TO PLANT A BALLED-AND-BURLAPPED TREE

B&B trees have a stronger root system and are usually easier to establish than container-grown trees, since they are grown in soil in the open ground rather than in soil mix in a container. However, the disadvantage is that some of the roots are invariably damaged on lifting; if the root ball breaks up, further damage is possible. Many evergreen trees, such as conifers, are grown in this way.

PLANTING TIPS

• Plant B&B trees as soon as possible after buying in autumn or early spring.
• Take great care when handling B&B trees. Aim to keep the root ball intact.
• If dry, water gently before planting, but never immerse in water.
• Shelter newly planted evergreens with windbreaks made from stakes and netting.

1 **Prepare the planting hole** as for container-grown trees (*see facing page*), but make the hole 2–3 times the diameter of the root ball. Place the tree in the hole and loosen the wrapping.

2 **Carefully remove** the wrapping by tilting the tree first to one side, then the other. Insert the stake or stakes now, if necessary. Backfill with the removed soil and organic matter. Firm, water, and mulch.

HOW TO PLANT A BARE-ROOT TREE

The advantage of bare-root trees is that they can be lifted with a considerable network of strong roots. Plant them as for container-grown trees (*see facing page*), but make the hole just wide enough to take the roots when spread out. Cut off any damaged roots before planting. Drive in a stake, then make a small mound of loose soil in the center of the hole. Place the tree on the mound, then spread out the roots.

1 **Using a stake**, line up the soil mark on the stem so that it is flush with the level of the surrounding soil.

2 **Gently firm** the soil to ensure that no large spaces are left around the roots. Water and mulch.

PLANTING TIPS

• Plant as soon as possible after purchase in autumn and early spring.
• Retain the covering around the roots until planting.
• If you can't plant the tree immediately, heel it in by covering the roots with moist soil in a trench until you are ready to plant.

How to Stake and Tie a Tree

Until the root systems are established, all but the smallest trees benefit from staking. The best stake is very sturdy and allows the head of the tree to move but keeps the base firm. In most cases, a low single stake is preferable. In windy sites, use a low angled stake or two stakes. High single stakes are needed only for trees with well-branched heads and a slender stem, such as crabapples (*Malus*); cut the stake down to a short stake after the first year. For strong support, use guy ropes (*see facing page*).

LOW STAKE
Use a low stake set vertically. For container-grown trees, set the stake at an angle of 45° leaning into the wind.

TWO STAKES
In windy conditions, use two vertical stakes, one on either side of the root ball (ideal for container-grown trees).

◄ BUCKLE-AND-SPACER TIE
This tie prevents the stake from rubbing against the tree and is adjustable to allow for growth. Tie it so that it is taut but will not damage the bark.

◄ RUBBER TIE
If you use a rubber tree tie without a buckle, nail it very firmly to the stake to prevent it from slipping and causing damage to the bark by friction.

Protecting the Stem

Deer, rabbits, and even scratching cats can cause irreversible harm to the bark of a young tree. If the damage is severe, the tree is likely to die. In some areas, it is vital to provide some form of protection for young trees. Spiral tree guards, made of flexible plastic that wraps around the stem, provide excellent protection, as do many other commercial guards available. Wire mesh, supported by stakes, is also highly effective. A barrier of netting that extends well below ground level will deter burrowing rabbits; insert it well clear of the roots.

SPIRAL STEM GUARD

WIRE MESH

TRANSPLANTING A YOUNG TREE

If you wish to move a tree, it is best to transplant it when it is small, up to about 8ft (2.5m) tall. Small trees are not only easier to move but are also quicker to establish in their new position. Larger trees may require professional attention.

Prepare the ground one year in advance of the planned move. In early autumn, mark out a circle around the tree with a diameter about one-third of the height of the tree. Outside the marked area, dig a trench 12in (30cm) wide and 24in (60cm) deep. Cut through any roots cleanly with a sharp spade, then undercut the tree as far as possible. Refill the trench with the soil mixed with organic matter.

1 **In autumn** the following year, dig another trench just outside the previous one to the same width and depth. Carefully fork away the soil from around the root ball.

2 **Taking care not** to damage the roots, undercut the root ball with a spade and, using pruners, cut back any awkward roots protruding from the root ball.

3 **Lay a piece** of burlap or plastic beside the tree. Tilting the tree first to one side and then the other, very carefully slide the sheet underneath the root ball.

4 **Bring up the sides** of the wrapping around the root ball. Tie it securely in place with ropes that pass around and underneath the root ball to keep intact.

5 **Move the tree** to its new site, lowering it into a predug planting hole (*see p.46*) using the ropes. Remove the wrapping, then replant the tree to the soil mark on the stem.

6 **When the tree** has been replanted, secure the tree with angled stakes and guy ropes. Water well and cover the ground around it with a 4in (10cm) layer of mulch.

PRUNING BASICS

YOUNG TREES, ESPECIALLY those that are deciduous, benefit from correct pruning and training to ensure the development of a well-shaped and balanced head. Mature trees, unless they are coppiced or pollarded (*see p.57*), usually require little pruning, although they may need to have the occasional wayward or crossing branches removed, or dead or diseased wood cut out.

CHOOSING THE RIGHT TOOL FOR THE JOB

Whichever job you are undertaking, selecting the appropriate tool makes the task easier, safer, and yields better results. The tool you use will depend on the size of the stem or branch that you intend to cut.

Invest in good-quality tools, and look after them properly. Keeping them clean and sharp is vital: a clean cut heals more quickly and is less liable to become infected.

Sharp cutting blade

Safety catch

Bright handles make them easy to find

Buffers prevent jarring when cutting

PRUNERS
Use pruners to cut woody shoots up to approximately ½in (1cm) thick, or for taking cuttings.

LOPPERS
For thick woody shoots ½–1in (1–2.5cm) thick, and for inaccessible stems, loppers are just right.

GARDEN KNIFE
A sharp, folding knife is useful for several tasks, such as light pruning, and for taking cuttings.

PRUNING SAW
Good for general-purpose pruning, this short-bladed saw can be used even in confined spaces.

LOOKING AFTER YOUR TOOLS
• Store tools in a dry place.
• After use, clean cutting blades by wiping with an oily rag or steel wool, dry well, then oil lightly.
• Keep blades sharp (saw blades should be sharpened by a professional).
• Replace any damaged blades when necessary.

DOUBLE-EDGED PRUNING SAW
This flexible saw has both coarse- and fine-toothed sides.

Clamp holds blade taut

BOW SAW
Ideal for cutting thick branches or even the trunk of a small tree.

How to Use Your Tools

Careful and correct use of pruning tools is vital for your safety and the health of the tree. Using tools incorrectly can result in poor cuts that damage the plant and may lead to infection and disease. The correct use of pruners, loppers, and a garden knife is shown below. For how to use a bow saw and pruning saw, see page 55.

PRUNERS
Use pruners with the thin cutting blade as close to the stem junction or bud as possible for a close cut.

LOPPERS
When using loppers, attempt to cut only shoots that will fit comfortably between the two blades.

GARDEN KNIFE
Smooth the rough edges of pruning cuts with a garden knife. This is essential to minimize infection.

Common Mistakes

Pruning incorrectly, by using a tool in the wrong way or by using one that is not suitable for the job, can damage both the plant and the tool. A common mistake is to try to use a single tool, such as pruners, for all pruning work, regardless of scale. Always use the right tool for the job, and never use the tool for any other purpose, such as cutting pieces of wire or lengths of string.

Thick blade is nearer the trunk, leaving a stub

Damaged tissue

INCORRECT USE
Cutting with pruners held the wrong way around, as here, can leave a stub that is liable to die back.

INCORRECT TOOL
This shoot is too thick to cut with pruners. Twisting them will damage both the plant and the pruners.

When and Where to Prune

The best time to prune most deciduous trees is in late autumn or winter. Other times are possible for most trees, except for maples (*Acer*), horse chestnuts (*Aesculus*), birches (*Betula*), and cherries (*Prunus*). Avoid pruning these in late winter or early spring, since they bleed sap when cut then. Prune all stems to just above a healthy bud: cutting too far above leaves a length of shoot that will die back, while cutting too close may damage the bud. The angle of cut depends on the position of the buds.

Straight cut

Angled cut

OPPOSITE BUDS
Where the buds are opposite, make a straight cut just above a pair of buds.

ALTERNATE BUDS
Where the buds are alternate, make an angled cut above a strong bud.

TRAINING YOUNG TREES

DECIDUOUS TREES are often sold already trained as "standards," with a clear stem and branched head. However, you can also buy them in "feathered" form, with side branches often to ground level, and train them yourself. This is both less expensive and more effective, since younger trees are quicker to establish than mature ones. The tree type will determine the training method.

FORMING A STANDARD TREE

The aim of this method, suitable for birches (*Betula*) for example, is to have a clear length of stem at the base by retaining the strong-growing central or leading shoot and removing the lower branches over two to three years.

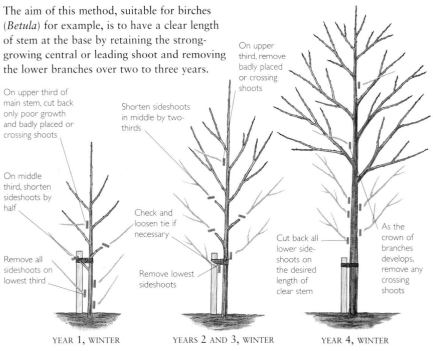

On upper third of main stem, cut back only poor growth and badly placed or crossing shoots

Shorten sideshoots in middle by two-thirds

On upper third, remove badly placed or crossing shoots

On middle third, shorten sideshoots by half

Check and loosen tie if necessary

Remove all sideshoots on lowest third

Remove lowest sideshoots

Cut back all lower side-shoots on the desired length of clear stem

As the crown of branches develops, remove any crossing shoots

YEAR 1, WINTER   YEARS 2 AND 3, WINTER   YEAR 4, WINTER

TRAINING A LEADING SHOOT

A single, straight leading shoot is essential if you are training a tree as a standard. If a competing leading shoot develops, remove it as soon as possible by cutting it off at the base. Where two or more leading shoots have been allowed to develop, select the strongest and straightest and remove its weaker competitor(s) (*see right*).

To replace a broken or damaged leading shoot, attach a stake to the main stem, then tie in another strong shoot (*see far right*). Prune back the broken shoot to the base.

SELECTING A LEADER   REPLACING A LEADER

FORMING A ROUND-HEADED TREE

For the first two or three years, train as for a standard tree (*see facing page*), then cut out the leading shoot. Suitable for most hawthorns (*Crataegus*), crabapples (*Malus*), and cherries (*Prunus*), this method will cause the tree to branch and spread horizontally.

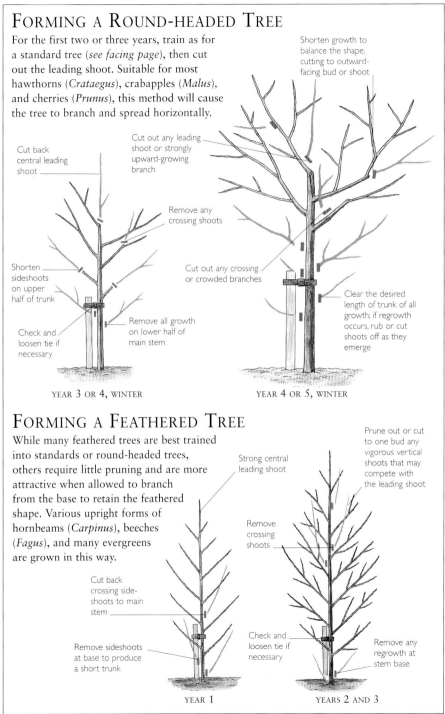

Shorten growth to balance the shape, cutting to outward-facing bud or shoot

Cut back central leading shoot

Cut out any leading shoot or strongly upward-growing branch

Remove any crossing shoots

Shorten sideshoots on upper half of trunk

Cut out any crossing or crowded branches

Check and loosen tie if necessary

Remove all growth on lower half of main stem

Clear the desired length of trunk of all growth; if regrowth occurs, rub or cut shoots off as they emerge

YEAR 3 OR 4, WINTER

YEAR 4 OR 5, WINTER

FORMING A FEATHERED TREE

While many feathered trees are best trained into standards or round-headed trees, others require little pruning and are more attractive when allowed to branch from the base to retain the feathered shape. Various upright forms of hornbeams (*Carpinus*), beeches (*Fagus*), and many evergreens are grown in this way.

Strong central leading shoot

Remove crossing shoots

Cut back crossing side-shoots to main stem

Remove sideshoots at base to produce a short trunk

Prune out or cut to one bud any vigorous vertical shoots that may compete with the leading shoot

Check and loosen tie if necessary

Remove any regrowth at stem base

YEAR 1

YEARS 2 AND 3

PRUNING MATURE TREES

GENERALLY, MATURE TREES require little pruning. However, when a tree becomes damaged or diseased, or causes an obstruction, action is needed. If a branch breaks, cut it back to an outward-facing bud on the same shoot or to its base. Cut diseased shoots back to a bud on healthy wood, which will show no discoloration when cut. If, after pruning, a shoot forms from a lower bud, leaving a stub of dead wood, cut this back to just above the new shoot.

REMOVING SUCKERS AND WATERSPROUTS

Many trees produce suckers, which are shoots that arise from the roots or the base of the trunk. These quickly become unsightly and take nutrients from the tree. Depending on their size, rub them off or cut them back to the base. More new suckers may be produced, which should be rubbed off as they appear. Watersprouts are unwanted, vigorous shoots that arise from the trunk or branches after pruning. Cut them back to the base with pruners.

SUCKERS
Cut suckers off where they arise, and rub off any new ones that may appear.

WATERSPROUTS
Watersprouts may arise from pruning wounds. Cut them off at the base.

CORRECTING UNEVEN GROWTH

If a small tree has grown to produce an unevenly shaped head, you can correct this by pruning. Prune the strong side lightly, and the weak side more heavily to stimulate growth of strong new shoots.

Prune growth on the weaker side hard

YEAR 1
In the first year, trim back the tips of the main branches on the strong side and prune the weaker side much harder. In the following years, remove only crossing shoots.

Tip-prune the main branches on the stronger side

PRECAUTIONS

• Carry out work only on small trees. Consult a professional tree surgeon for larger ones.

• Work from the ground whenever possible, and take care if using ladders or climbing the tree.

• Never attempt to climb the tree when the bark is wet and slippery.

• Keep the area around the tree clear of equipment, children, and pets.

• If using a chain saw, do so from the ground, and never on branches above waist height.

• Before undertaking any work, always consult your local government. The tree may be legally protected, and you may need permission for felling or even simply removing branches.

Cutting Off a Branch

It is vital to exercise particular care when cutting a branch off a tree. It can be dangerous and, if done incorrectly, may damage the tree. A branch over 4in (10cm) in diameter is best removed in stages. The use of two cuts prevents any tearing of the bark when the cut portion falls.

Make the final cut just outside the branch collar, the swelling at the branch base, where the tree's natural defenses are located. Keeping this cut clean and smooth minimizes the risk of infection entering the tree, so clean the edges of the cut with a sharp knife. Do not paint the cut surface.

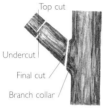

Top cut

Undercut

Final cut

Branch collar

WHERE TO CUT
When making final cuts, avoid damaging the branch collar at the base of the branch, since this area protects the tree from infection.

1 Using a pruning saw, make the first cut from beneath the branch, about 12in (30cm) from the trunk and about one-quarter of the way through the branch.

2 Remove the outer portion of the branch by cutting through from above, about 1in (2.5cm) farther from the trunk than the original cut.

3 To cut off the stub, make a small undercut from below, then saw from above, angling the saw slightly away from the trunk, until the two cuts meet.

Cutting Down a Small Tree

Felling a tree can be a very hazardous activity. If you need to cut down a tree in your yard, tackle only those up to 15ft (5m) tall. To fell larger trees, you will need to seek the services of a professional tree surgeon. A bow saw is useful for felling small trees, but it may be difficult to use in

confined areas. Trees are best taken down in stages. Before you begin, ensure that there is sufficient space for the tree to fall safely. Remove the larger branches, then make three cuts as shown below, the first two on the side where the tree is to fall. Finally, dig out the stump and roots.

1 Using a bow saw, make an angled cut one-third into the trunk on the side where the tree is to fall. The cut should be about 3ft (1m) from the ground.

2 Make a horizontal cut to meet the base of the angled cut. Remove the wedge of wood. This will ensure that the tree falls in the planned direction when cut.

3 Make the final cut on the opposite side, just above the wedge. Push the tree as it starts to fall. Dig a trench around the remaining stump and dig or pull it out.

PRUNING FOR SPECIAL EFFECT

CERTAIN TREES GROWN FOR their ornamental shoots and bark can be greatly enhanced by special pruning techniques, such as pollarding and coppicing. These encourage the production of vigorous new growth and also restrict the size of the plant, keeping the ornamental features at eye level. Some evergreen trees, such as hollies (*Ilex*), bay (*Laurus*), and yew (*Taxus*), are suited to training as standards (*see pp.52–53*). Remove the lower branches to the desired height, then prune in spring before growth starts until you achieve the desired shape. Trim mature plants regularly but lightly in summer.

CREATING MULTISTEMMED TREES

Many trees naturally produce several stems from the base; for those that do not, you can encourage a multistemmed habit by pruning. This is particularly desirable for trees with ornamental bark or shoots, since it shows them to best effect. Examples of trees that are suited to growing as multi-stemmed specimens include *Acer davidii* and other snakebark maples, birches (*Betula*), *Cercis*, and *Lagerstroemia*.

▶ MULTISTEMMED MAPLE
Growing Acer pensylvanicum *'Erythrocladum' as a multistemmed tree makes it stronger and creates more young shoots for winter effect.*

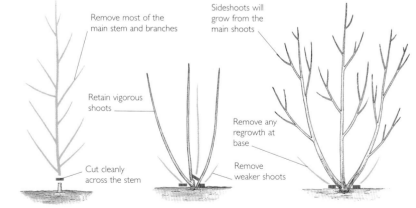

Remove most of the main stem and branches

Sideshoots will grow from the main shoots

Retain vigorous shoots

Remove any regrowth at base

Remove weaker shoots

Cut cleanly across the stem

YEAR 1, WINTER
Cut the main stem of a 2-year-old tree at least 3in (8cm) from the ground, more if desired. Trim sharp edges.

YEAR 2, WINTER
Choose approximately 3 strong, well-spaced shoots of equal vigor. Cut all other shoots back to the base.

YEAR 3, WINTER
Allow sideshoots to develop, cutting only the lower ones if you want clear stems. Remove any suckers that may appear.

POLLARDING AND COPPICING

These pruning techniques restrict growth and encourage the production of vigorous young shoots for winter or foliage effect. Among the best trees for pollarding are forms of the white willow (*Salix alba*). To pollard a tree, first let it develop until well established and growing strongly. Just before growth starts in spring, reduce it to the required stem height by sawing across the main stem. Cut the remaining shoots back to 1–3in (2.5–8cm) long.

Coppicing is similar, but the tree is cut down to just above ground level. This creates a shrubby effect, with many shoots arising from the base. It is often used on hazel (*Corylus avellana*) but can also be applied to some large trees, such as some maples (*Acer*) and *Paulownia tomentosa*, encouraging the production of vigorous shoots and very large leaves.

▲ STRIKING STEMS
Regular pollarding of the willow Salix alba *'Britzensis' produces a head of vigorous red shoots that makes a striking feature in the garden in winter and early spring.*

◀ CUTTING BACK
The variegated forms of Acer negundo *can be cut back hard in spring to encourage a bushy habit and to restrict their size.*

VARIEGATED NEW LEAVES
The maple Acer negundo *'Flamingo' responds extremely well to hard pruning. Shown here pollarded to a low stem, it produces numerous vigorous shoots that bear large, attractively variegated young leaves, making a more handsome plant than if left unpruned.*

POLLARDING TIPS

• Prune established pollards every 2–3 years.
• Carry out pollarding in early spring so that the ornamental effects can be enjoyed over winter.
• Remove any shoots on the main stem below the head or at the base of the tree as they appear.
• When growth starts, the shoots may be overcrowded. Remove some if necessary to create an even head of branches.

PESTS, DISEASES, AND DISORDERS

MANY TREES enjoy a healthy life. Some, however, will suffer at some time from pests, diseases, or disorders. Pests are generally insects or other creatures that feed on parts of a tree; diseases are caused by fungi, bacteria, or viruses; and disorders are usually the result of poor growing conditions. A healthy, well-maintained tree will be considerably more resistant to problems of all kinds than one that is in poor condition.

PREVENTING PROBLEMS

Buy a good, healthy specimen that is suited to the conditions in your garden. Plant it correctly, and water and weed regularly. Prune as little as possible, use clean, sharp tools, and avoid wounding stems (for example, when using a lawn mower). If diseased material is found on other woody plants in the garden, remove and discard it immediately. Check regularly for signs of pests and diseases, and take immediate action if a problem occurs.

MOTTLING
Tiny spider mites feed on the foliage, causing a dull mottling on the surface and leaf fall. Wash off with water or use a pesticide.

Susceptible trees: maples (*Acer*), crabapples (*Malus*), spruce (*Picea*), and willows (*Salix*).

Distorted growth

STUNTED LEAVES
Aphids suck sap and leave a sticky deposit. Wash off with water or use a suitable pesticide as soon as seen.

Susceptible trees: maples (*Acer*), hawthorns (*Crataegus*), beech (*Fagus*), crabapples (*Malus*), *Prunus, Sorbus.*

GALLS
Unsightly growths (galls) form, usually on the leaves, as a response to feeding by insects or mites. No effective control, but no real harm is done.

Susceptible trees: maples (*Acer*), beech (*Fagus*), *Gleditsia triacanthos* 'Sunburst', oaks (*Quercus*), elms (*Ulmus*).

CHEWED LEAVES
Caterpillars can quickly eat through foliage. Gather any caterpillars on the tree's leaves; alternatively, use pesticides for serious infestations.

Susceptible trees: maples (*Acer*), hornbeams (*Carpinus*), bay (*Laurus*), crabapples (*Malus*), *Prunus, Sorbus.*

SHRIVELED LEAVES
Drought causes leaves to wilt, shrivel, or color early. Prevent this by watering the tree regularly, especially in the year after planting. Mulch newly planted trees.

Susceptible trees: all trees may be affected, especially those that have been newly planted or grown in containers.

CONGESTED SHOOTS
Dense clusters of congested shoots are produced on branches in response to insect or fungal attack. Cut back affected shoots to normal wood.

Susceptible trees: birches (*Betula*), hornbeams (*Carpinus*), *Prunus*.

Dead bark covered in pustules

PUSTULES ON BARK
Colored spots of fungus usually appear on dead shoots but can harm live wood. Cut affected shoots back to unmarked, healthy wood.

Susceptible trees: horse chestnuts (*Aesculus*), hornbeams (*Carpinus*), *Cercis*, magnolias, sumacs (*Rhus*).

FUNGUS
White growth and black strands under the bark of trunks and roots indicate honey fungus. Remove and destroy infected root systems.

Susceptible trees: Birches (*Betula*), *Chamaecyparis*, *Cupressus*, magnolias, crabapples (*Malus*), *Prunus*, pears (*Pyrus*).

RUPTURED BARK
Rapid uptake of water after a prolonged drought causes stems to swell suddenly, splitting the bark. Water regularly in dry spells.

Susceptible trees: all trees are affected, but especially those growing in containers or in soil that dries out quickly.

WOUNDED BARK
Mechanical damage or incorrect or unclean pruning cuts can damage trunks. Ensure stakes do not rub, and prune trees correctly (pp.51, 55).

Susceptible trees: all trees are affected, but especially those grown in grass, which are liable to damage by lawn mowers.

Stem may split and eventually die back

CRACKED STEM
Extremely low temperatures or sudden temperature changes cause stems to freeze and split. Grow tender trees in a sheltered position.

Susceptible trees: many trees are affected, but especially young or slightly tender ones, and in particular those growing in exposed sites.

OTHER COMMON PROBLEMS

LEAVES AND FLOWERS

White powder on leaves Powdery mildew causes leaves to fall early. Water well and spray with fungicide.

Leaf spots Bacteria or fungi cause blotches on leaves. Remove and discard affected foliage as soon as seen.

Eaten flower buds Birds may eat the flower buds of some trees in winter, especially those of *Prunus* or any other tree with large buds.

SHOOTS

Eaten bark and shoots Deer and rabbits eat the shoots, bark, and foliage of trees, so use a stem guard for protection (*p.48*).

White fluff on conifers A sign of aphidlike insects (adelgids), which suck sap from the leaves and shoots. Spray with a pesticide.

Brown scales with white egg deposits Scale insects feed on the shoots and leaves of many trees. Control by spraying with a pesticide.

RECOMMENDED SMALL TREES

THE SYMBOLS AND HEIGHTS given in this plant directory apply to all trees described in the entry unless otherwise stated. If acidic soil is not specified, assume the tree is suitable for any reasonably good, well-drained soil.

▦ *Shade tolerant* ▧ *Suitable for sun or partial shade* ▨ *Best in full sun* ◊ *Tolerates dry soil* ◊ *Requires moist, well-drained soil* ♦ *Tolerates wet soil Hardiness zone ranges are given as* **Zx–x** **H** *Approximate maximum height growing in cultivation in reasonable conditions*

A

Abies koreana
(Korean fir)
Evergreen, narrowly conical conifer with densely arranged, glossy dark green leaves, bright blue-white beneath. Small, blue-purple cones are borne even on small plants. It is best grown in acidic soil.
▧ ◊ **Z5–6 H** 30ft (10m)

ABIES KOREANA

Abies lasiocarpa var. *arizonica* 'Compacta'
This slow-growing, very compact, narrowly columnar evergreen conifer needs acidic soil. It has dense, bright blue-gray foliage.
▨ ◊ **Z5–6 H** 15ft (5m)

Aesculus × *neglecta* 'Erythroblastos'
(Sunrise horse chestnut)
Deciduous, broadly columnar tree (*p.26*). The leaves are brilliant pink in spring, turning green flushed yellow then green in summer. The creamy white flowers, which are borne in late spring, are inconspicuous.
▧ ◊ **Z5–8 H** 25ft (8m)

Aesculus pavia
(Red buckeye)
Deciduous, broadly conical tree (*p.30*), which bears tubular red flowers in early summer. 'Atrosanguinea' has deep red flowers. The forms of *A.* × *mutabilis*, such as 'Induta' and 'Penduliflora',
are similar but more bushy, with pink flowers marked with yellow.
▨ **Z5–8 H** 20ft (6m)

Albizia julibrissin f. *rosea*
(Mimosa, Silk tree)
Deciduous, rounded to spreading tree. It has elegant, fernlike leaves and showy pink powderpuff-like clusters in summer.
▨ ◊ **Z6–9 H** 20ft (6m)

AESCULUS PAVIA
'ATROSANGUINEA'

◀ MALUS 'RED JADE' *The white flowers of this crabapple are magnificent in late spring.*

ACER (MAPLE)

Maples form a diverse group, from shrubs to large trees. All have excellent foliage and provide some of the best trees for autumn color. Many also have interesting bark or shoots, or an attractive habit. The following are all deciduous, and the majority are rounded or spreading.
🅰 ◊ Hardiness varies
H 30ft (10m)

Maples with attractive bark or shoots

The snakebark maples are fast-growing trees with green- and white-streaked bark and good autumn color. They include *A. capillipes* (**Z5–7**, *p.17*), *A. davidii* (**Z5–7**, some of which, including '**Ernest Wilson**', color orange in autumn), and *A. rufinerve* (**Z6–9**). Another attractive snakebark maple is *A. pensylvanicum* (Moosewood, **Z3–7**, *p.29*), with yellow leaves in autumn; '**Erythrocladum**' (*p.56*) has bright pink winter shoots.

Other maples grown for their bark or shoots include: *A. buergerianum* (Trident maple, **Z5–9**), with orange-brown flaking bark and red autumn color; *A. griseum* (Paperbark maple, **Z4–8**, *p.28*), with striking peeling cinnamon-brown bark; *A. palmatum* '**Senkaki**', syn. '**Sango-kaku**' (Coralbark maple, **Z6–8**, *pp.28, 38*), with shoots coral-red in winter; *A. triflorum* (**Z5–7**, *p.27*), with pale gray-brown peeling bark and brilliant orange autumn color.

Maples grown for foliage

A. cappadocicum '**Aureum**' (**Z6–8**) has yellow foliage that turns a little greener in summer. Good cultivars of *A. japonicum* (**Z5–7**) include '**Aconitifolium**', with deeply cut leaves, which is slightly shrubby, to 15ft (5m); '**Vitifolium**' is larger, with bigger, less divided leaves. Both turn bright red in autumn. The leaves of *A. negundo* '**Flamingo**' (*pp.17, 57*) have a strong pink flush on their edges when young; '**Variegatum**' has leaves that are edged white (both **Z5–8**). The foliage of *A. palmatum* (**Z6–8**, *pp.17, 34*) turns orange, red, or yellow in autumn. Selections include '**Atropurpureum**', with purple leaves; '**Linearilobum**', with the leaves cut into slender lobes;

'**Ôsakazuki**', with large leaves, red in autumn; and '**Shishigashira**', broadly columnar, to 15ft (5m), with small, sharply toothed leaves. *A. pseudoplatanus* '**Brilliantissimum**' (**Z4–7**, *p.40*) has bright pink young foliage. *A. rubrum* '**Schlesingeri**' (**Z3–9**) colors early in autumn, very bright red. *A. shirasawanum* '**Aureum**' (**Z5–7**, *pp.8, 27*) has bright yellow foliage. *A. tataricum* subsp. *ginnala* (**Z3–7**) has glossy leaves, turning red in autumn.

Maples grown for their habit

Acer campestre (Hedge maple, **Z5–8**) grows to 25ft (8m) and makes a dense screen. Several forms of Japanese maple, *A. palmatum* (**Z6–8**), are grown as weeping trees, 8–10ft (2.5–3m) tall. Dissectum Group cultivars have finely cut leaves turning orange to red in autumn, such as '**Crimson Queen**', with red-purple foliage, or the green-leaved var. *dissectum*. *A. saccharum* '**Newton Sentry**' (**Z4–8**) is narrowly columnar, with orange-red autumn color.

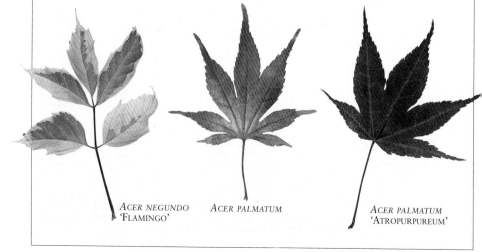

ACER NEGUNDO
'FLAMINGO'

ACER PALMATUM

ACER PALMATUM
'ATROPURPUREUM'

ARBUTUS × ANDRACHNOIDES

Alnus glutinosa 'Imperialis'

This form of the black alder is a graceful, broadly conical deciduous tree, which has finely cut dark green leaves arranged on slightly drooping shoots. Needs permanently moist soil.
▨ ◗ Z3–7 H 30ft (10m)

Alnus incana 'Aurea'

Deciduous, broadly columnar tree with orange-pink shoots and young catkins in winter that create the effect of a pink haze. It has yellow-green young foliage. 'Pendula', another form of *A. incana*, is weeping in habit.
▨ ◗◗ Z2–6 H 30ft (10m)

Amelanchier

(Serviceberry)
Deciduous, rounded or spreading, sometimes shrubby trees that require acidic soil. They have attractive young foliage that turns orange to red in autumn, white spring flowers, and blue-black fruits. *A. arborea* (Z4–9) and *A. lamarckii* (Z5–9, *p.22*) both have silvery young leaves. *A.* × *grandiflora*

(Z5–8), including its forms 'Autumn Brilliance' and 'Ballerina', as well as *A. laevis* (Z5–9), have bronze young foliage.
▨▨ ◗ H 25–30ft (8–10m)

Aralia elata

(Japanese angelica tree)
Deciduous, suckering shrub or broadly columnar tree with spiny stems, large divided leaves, and a gaunt winter profile. Small white flowers appear in late summer as the leaves turn orange, yellow, and purple; small black fruits follow. The similar *A. spinosa* flowers in early summer.
▨ ◗ Z4–9 H 30ft (10m)

Arbutus

These spreading, evergreen trees, sometimes shrubby in habit, produce particularly attractive fruits and bark. *A.* × *andrachnoides* (Z8–9) has cinnamon-brown peeling bark and small white flowers from autumn to spring. *A. unedo* (Strawberry tree, Z7–9) bears small white flowers, pink in f. *rubra*, and strawberry-like fruits in autumn and winter. It also has rough-textured, reddish brown bark.
▨ ◗ H 25ft (8m)

B

Betula pendula

(European white birch)
Narrowly conical, deciduous tree with white bark and weeping shoots. 'Laciniata' produces finely cut leaves; 'Tristis' has long, pendulous shoots. 'Youngii', to 25ft (8m), has a mushroom-shaped head, and shoots to the ground.
▨ ◗ Z2–7 H 70ft (20m) or more

Betula populifolia

(Gray birch)
Deciduous, narrowly conical tree with reddish brown bark becoming white or gray. The slender shoots are somewhat pendulous, and the glossy dark green leaves turn yellow in autumn.
▨ ◗ Z3–6 H 30ft (10m)

Betula utilis var. jacquemontii

(Himalayan birch)
Vigorous deciduous, narrowly columnar tree (*pp.29, 36*) with white bark. It bears long catkins in spring and has golden yellow autumn color. 'Jermyns' is a form with particularly attractive, pure white bark.
▨ ◗ Z5–7 H 50ft (15m)

Buddleja alternifolia

Deciduous, weeping shrub (*p.10*), which is sometimes available as a weeping standard. It has slender, gray-green leaves. In early summer, clusters of fragrant lilac flowers are borne along the branches. Mature specimens have attractive flaking bark.
▨ ◗ Z6–9 H 10ft (3m)

BETULA PENDULA 'TRISTIS'

C

Calocedrus decurrens 'Berrima Gold'

Evergreen, narrowly columnar conifer, a slow-growing form of the large incense cedar. It has bright yellow, aromatic foliage turning orange-yellow in winter, and orange bark.
◼ ◊ Z5–8 H 20ft (6m)

Caragana arborescens

(Siberian pea tree)
Deciduous, broadly columnar shrub with divided leaves and yellow flowers in spring. The following are usually grown as standards: **'Lorbergii'**, with slender, arching shoots and very finely cut leaves, and **'Pendula'**, which is not usually above 5ft (1.5m), often less, and has stiff, strongly weeping shoots.
◼ ◊ Z2–8 H 10ft (3m)

Carpinus

(Hornbeam)
Hornbeams are deciduous trees grown for their elegant habit, foliage, autumn color, and fruits. *C. betulus*

CATALPA BIGNONIOIDES 'AUREA'

(Hornbeam, Z4–8) has sharply toothed leaves turning yellow in autumn and is 30ft (10m) tall. **'Columnaris'** (*p.12*) is compact and narrowly columnar; **'Fastigiata'** becomes large and requires pruning to keep it narrow, while **'Frans Fontaine'** retains its narrow shape; **'Pendula'** is a mushroom-headed tree, to 8ft (2.5m) tall, the branches weeping to the ground.
C. caroliniana (American hornbeam, Blue beech, Musclewood, Z3–9) is larger, occasionally reaching 40ft (12m) tall, sometimes shrubby, and rounded to spreading. Its autumn leaves are yellow or orange, and green fruit clusters hang beneath the branches in summer, turning yellow-brown.
◼◾ ◊

Catalpa bignonioides 'Aurea'

(Indian bean tree)
Deciduous, rounded to spreading tree with large golden leaves, which appear late. Bears large heads of white flowers in summer, followed by long, slender, persistent pods.
◼◾ ◊ Z5–9 H 25ft (8m)

Cercis

Deciduous, rounded to spreading trees with small, usually pink flowers that appear before the leaves open. Mature trees often bear flowers on the main trunk and branches. *C. canadensis* **'Forest Pansy'** (Eastern redbud, Z5–9) has purple foliage. *C. chinensis* (Z6–9) reaches only 20ft (6m) high, with glossy foliage, and **'Avondale'** is even more compact at 10ft (3m).
C. siliquastrum (Judas tree,

Z6–9, *p.11*) produces pink or occasionally white flowers.
◼ ◊ H 30ft (10m)

Chamaecyparis

(Cypress)
This is a group of narrowly columnar conifers. Forms of *C. lawsoniana* (Lawson cypress, Z5–9) include **'Columnaris'** and **'Ellwoodii'**, both with blue-gray foliage. Selections of *C. obtusa* (Z4–8) include **'Crippsii'** (*p.13*), with sprays of golden-yellow foliage, and **'Tetragona Aurea'**, which has clustered golden to bronze-yellow foliage.
C. pisifera **'Boulevard'** (Z4–8) has soft blue-gray leaves.
C. thyoides **'Andeleyensis'** (Z3–8) is dense and narrow, with blue-green foliage and reaches 15–20ft (5–6m) tall.
◼ ◊ H 30ft (10m)

Chionanthus

(Fringe tree)
Deciduous or evergreen trees grown for their flowers and fruits. *C. retusus* (Z6–8) is deciduous, with fragrant white summer flowers, small blue-black fruits that follow in

CHAMAECYPARIS OBTUSA 'CRIPPSII'

CHIONANTHUS VIRGINICUS

autumn, and attractive flaking bark. *C. virginicus* (Z5–8), also deciduous, is grown for its large clusters of fragrant white flowers in summer, followed by small, blue-black fruits. Needs acidic soil.
◫ H 10–12ft (3–4m)

Cordyline australis
(New Zealand cabbage palm) Evergreen, palmlike tree (*p.35*) with a dense head of slender leaves. Large clusters of small, white, fragrant, summer flowers are followed by tiny white or blue-tinged berries. **'Albertii'** has cream leaves edged pink; **'Atropurpurea'** has purple-flushed foliage; **'Torbay Dazzler'** has leaves striped cream; **'Variegata'** has leaves striped creamy white.
◫ ◊ Z10–11 H 30ft (10m)

Cotinus obovatus
(American smoke tree) Deciduous, broadly conical shrub or small tree with platelike brown bark and oval leaves that turn brilliant orange, red, and purple in autumn. "Smoky" fruit clusters persist into autumn.
◫ ◊ Z4–8 H 30ft (10m)

CORNUS (DOGWOOD)

Dogwoods are grown for their flowers, fruit, elegant habit, and autumn color. They are mainly rounded and spreading deciduous shrubs and small trees.
◫ ◊ Hardiness varies

Flowering dogwoods
The flowering dogwoods are those with very large bracts. *C. capitata* is evergreen but is suitable only for Zones 8–9. It reaches 30ft (10m) tall and across. The bracts emerge creamy yellow and may become flushed pink. Bears strawberry-like fruits in autumn. *C.* **'Eddie's White Wonder'** (Z5–8) has white bracts and needs acidic soil. It reaches 20ft (6m). *C. florida* (Z5–8) is a spreading tree, sometimes shrubby, growing to 20ft (6m). There are many forms, with bracts ranging from deep pink in **'Cherokee Chief'** to white in **'White Cloud'**, opening in late spring to early summer. Needs acidic soil. *C. kousa* (Z5–8) is similar to *C. florida* but will grow in alkaline soil. It has creamy bracts in early to midsummer, peeling bark, and

CORNUS MAS

red autumn color. It reaches 20ft (6m). Among the best forms are var. *chinensis*, with large bracts, and **'Satomi'**, with red bracts.
C. x *rutgersensis* Stellar Series (Z5–8) are vigorous, disease-resistant hybrids of *C. florida* and *C. kousa*, growing to 30ft (10m).

Other dogwoods
C. alternifolia (Pagoda dogwood, Z4–8) grows to 20ft (6m). It has distinctive tiered branches, small white summer flowers, and leaves that turn red and purple in autumn. *C. controversa* **'Variegata'** (Z6–9) is similar, to 25ft (8m) tall and across, and with larger, white-margined leaves. *C. macrophylla* (Z7–8) is broadly conical, to 30ft (10m), with bold dark green leaves, broad heads of small white flowers in late summer, and small blue-black fruits. *C. mas* (Cornelian cherry, Z5–8) is often shrubby but may be treelike, up to 25ft (8m). Small yellow flowers open on the bare branches in late winter and are often followed by edible red fruits.

CORNUS FLORIDA
'CHEROKEE CHIEF'

CRATAEGUS LAEVIGATA
'PAUL'S SCARLET'

for their flowers, such as 'Crimson Cloud', red with a white eye, and 'Paul's Scarlet', double and deep pink. The semi-evergreen C. × *lavallei* 'Carrierei' (Z5–7) has orange-red fruits lasting into winter. C. *pedicellata* (Z6–8) has large red fruits. C. *phaenopyrum* (Washington hawthorn, Z4–8) has maplelike leaves, red in autumn, and produces small orange-red fruits. C. *viridis* 'Winter King' (Z5–7) has long-lasting red fruits.
◼ ◊◊ H 25ft (8m)

Cotoneaster
The following cotoneasters may be available as weeping standards. C. 'Herbstfeuer' (syn. C. 'Autumn Fire', Z5–8), has glossy evergreen leaves and red berries.
C. *integrifolius* (syn. C. *microphyllus*, Z6–8), has tiny, dark green, evergreen leaves; rigid, arching shoots; and crimson-pink fruits.
C. 'Hybridus Pendulus' (syn. C. *salicifolius* 'Pendulus', Z6–8) is semievergreen, to 6ft (2m), with profuse red berries.
◼ ◊◊ H 4–5ft (1.2–1.5m)

Crataegus
(Hawthorn)
Hawthorns are deciduous, rounded to spreading trees, usually thorny and with white flowers in early summer.
C. *crus-galli* (Cockspur hawthorn, Z4–7) has long, curved spines, persistent red fruits, and red autumn color.
C. *laciniata* (Z6–8, *p.38*) has lobed dark green leaves and orange-red fruits. Forms of C. *laevigata* (English hawthorn, Z5–8) are grown

Cupressus
(Cypress)
These are evergreen, narrowly conical conifers.
C. *arizonica* 'Pyramidalis' (Z7–9) may sometimes exceed 30ft (10m), but it is compact with attractive blue-gray foliage. Forms of the Italian cypress, C. *sempervirens* (Z8–10), such as 'Green Pencil' and 'Stricta', 20ft (6m), make good dark green, formal specimens. 'Swane's Gold', to 20ft (6m), has golden foliage.
◼ ◊

EMBOTHRIUM COCCINEUM

ERIOBOTRYA JAPONICA

E

Elaeagnus angustifolia
(Oleaster, Russian olive)
Deciduous, spreading shrub or tree (*p.32*), valued since it grows in poor, dry soils. It has slender, willowlike, silvery leaves and tiny scented yellow summer flowers. Has become an invasive weed in some areas.
◼ ◊ Z3–8 H 25ft (8m)

Embothrium coccineum
(Chilean fire bush)
Deciduous or semievergreen, broadly columnar tree that needs acidic soil. It bears showy, bright red flowers in late spring and early summer among the narrow dark green leaves.
◼ ◊ Z8–10 H 30ft (10m)

Eriobotrya japonica
(Loquat)
Evergreen, rounded to spreading tree or shrub. Its small fragrant white flowers open in autumn or winter. Where summers are hot or winters mild, it will produce edible, orange-yellow fruits.
◼ ◊ Z8–10 H 25ft (8m)

Eucryphia glutinosa
This deciduous or semi-evergreen, broadly columnar tree needs acidic soil. It produces glossy, dark green leaves, orange-red in autumn, and large white, slightly fragrant flowers that open in mid- to late summer.
▣ ◊ Z8–10 H 30ft (10m)

F

Fagus sylvatica
(European beech)
This deciduous tree has several forms that are suitable for small gardens. 'Aurea Pendula' is slender and narrowly columnar, with pendulous branches hanging against the trunk and yellow foliage. 'Dawyck Gold' is also narrowly columnar, with yellow foliage becoming green, then turning yellow again in autumn. 'Purple Fountain' is similar to 'Aurea Pendula', but with purple foliage, while 'Purpurea Pendula' (p.20) is weeping, to only 10ft (3m), and has deep purple leaves.
▣ ◊ Z5–7 H 30ft (10m)

FRANKLINIA ALATAMAHA

Ficus carica
(Common fig)
This deciduous tree, often shrubby, has a spreading head of bold, deeply lobed leaves. The edible fruits can be up to 4in (10cm) long. 'Brown Turkey' has purple fruits. In cold climates it is best grown against a sunny wall.
▣ ◊ Z6–9 H 15ft (5m)

Franklinia alatamaha
(Franklin tree)
Rounded or spreading deciduous tree or shrub. This has glossy dark green leaves, which are bright red in autumn. In late summer, large, cup-shaped, fragrant white flowers open. It does best in acidic soil.
▣ ◊ Z6–9 H 15ft (5m)

G

Genista aetnensis
(Mount Etna broom)
Almost leafless, the green stems of this rounded to spreading, deciduous tree give it an evergreen appearance. In late summer, it is covered in small, fragrant, bright yellow flowers.
▣ ◊ Z9–10 H 25ft (8m)

Gleditsia triacanthos 'Sunburst'
This deciduous tree is broadly conical in habit. It is fast growing and may exceed 30ft (10m) tall. It is grown for its elegant, fernlike foliage, which is bright yellow when young and dark green in maturity, turning yellow in autumn. Like most of the cultivars, this form is thornless.
▣ ◊ Z3–7 H 30ft (10m)

H

Halesia
(Silverbell)
These are deciduous trees that require an acidic soil. Broadly conical or columnar in outline, they branch low from the base. In late spring, they bear white, bell-shaped flowers, and in autumn they produce green, winged fruits. H. diptera (Z5–8) is about 25ft (8m), and frequently shrubby; H. monticola (Z6–9) often exceeds 30ft (10m). It has a pink-flowered form, f. rosea.
▣ ◊

Hydrangea paniculata
Vigorous, spreading, deciduous shrub that is sometimes trained as a standard. Produces attractive, large flowerheads in late summer and autumn. Recommended selections include 'Grandiflora' and 'Unique', with large white flowerheads turning pink. 'Praecox' flowers relatively early, and 'Tardiva' is a late-flowering form.
▣ ◊ Z4–8 H 10ft (3m)

HALESIA MONTICOLA

ILEX (HOLLY)

Hollies include some of the most popular evergreens, valued for their foliage and berries. Unless otherwise stated, the following are female with red berries, and narrowly conical in habit. Berries are produced only if a male plant is growing nearby.
▣ ◊ Hardiness varies
H 15–20ft (5–6m)

English hollies (Z7–9)
Forms of *I. aquifolium* include 'Argentea Marginata Pendula', weeping, to 8ft (2.5m), with cream-edged leaves; '**Golden Milkboy**', male, with leaves blotched yellow; '**Green Pillar**', a narrowly upright form; '**Handsworth New Silver**', with purple shoots and white-edged leaves; '**Madame Briot**', with purple stems and yellow-edged leaves, to 30ft (10m); the male '**Ovata Aurea**', with purple shoots and gold-edged leaves; '**Pyramidalis Fructu Luteo**', with yellow berries and mostly spineless leaves; and '**Silver Milkmaid**', with spiny white-blotched leaves.
    Similar to English hollies are forms of *I.* × *altaclerensis*. Selections include '**Belgica Aurea**', with yellow-edged leaves, the margin becoming

ILEX AQUIFOLIUM
'SILVER MILKMAID'

creamy white, to 30ft (10m) or more; '**Camelliifolia Variegata**', with leaves broadly edged yellow; '**Golden King**' (*p.33*), with yellow-edged leaves; and '**Lawsoniana**', with leaves blotched yellow and pale green in the center.

Other hollies
I. × *attenuata* (Topel holly, Z6–9) is bushy, with narrow, spiny leaves and red berries on female plants. *I. latifolia* (Z7–9), to 25ft (8m), has long, bold, dark green leaves; red fruits on female plants may persist in winter. *I.* × *koehneana* (Z7–9), is similar with smaller, spinier leaves. *I.* '**Nellie R. Stevens**' (Z7–9), is conical, to 22ft (7m), with very spiny leaves and red fruits. *I. opaca* (American holly, Z5–9), to 30ft (10m), has matte to glossy, pale to dark green, spiny foliage. It prefers hot summers and acidic soil. *I. pedunculosa* (Z6–9), 22ft (7m), has wavy-edged, spineless leaves, bronze when young, and long-stalked red berries on female plants.

ILEX PEDUNCULOSA

I–J

Illicium anisatum
(Chinese anise)
This is a conical, evergreen shrub or small tree with oval, glossy, dark green leaves. Star-shaped, fragrant, yellow-green to white flowers bloom in spring. Aromatic, starlike fruits follow. Needs acidic soil.
▣ ◊ Z7–9 H 25ft (8m)

Juniperus chinensis
(Chinese juniper)
Evergreen conifer with forms including '**Aurea**', which is narrow and slow growing, with bright yellow foliage; '**Kaizuka**' (Hollywood juniper), to 20ft (6m), with irregularly spreading shoots and profuse, bloomy berries; '**Spartan**', which is a narrow column of bright green.
▣ ◊ Z3–9 H 30ft (10m)

Juniperus scopulorum
'**Skyrocket**'
One of the narrowest of all conifers, with blue-gray evergreen foliage.
▣ ◊ Z4–7 H 20ft (6m)

KOELREUTERIA PANICULATA

K

Koelreuteria paniculata
(Golden rain tree, Pride of India)
Deciduous tree of spreading habit, with leaves emerging bronze-red, turning green, then orange or yellow in autumn. Large clusters of yellow flowers open in summer, turning to green or pink, later with brown, lanternlike fruits. 'Fastigiata' has upright branches.
◻ ◊ **Z6–9** H 30ft (10m)

L

Laburnum
(Golden chain tree)
These deciduous trees are excellent as specimens for small gardens. They are grown for their long, pendulous clusters of bright yellow flowers in late spring and early summer. All parts of laburnums are highly toxic if they are eaten. *L. alpinum* 'Pendulum' (Z5–8) is a weeping tree, 5ft (1.5m) tall.

LAGERSTROEMIA INDICA 'SEMINOLE'

LAURUS NOBILIS 'AUREA'

L. × *watereri* 'Vossii' (Z6–8, p.25) is broadly columnar and considerably taller, to 25ft (8m) high.
◻ ◊

Lagerstroemia indica
(Crape myrtle)
Deciduous, broadly spreading tree or shrub with peeling bark and profuse flowers in large clusters in summer and autumn. Flowers are white to pink, red, or purple. Most of the following resist powdery mildew. 'Catawba' bears purple flowers; foliage turns orange-red in autumn. 'Cherokee' has bright red flowers. 'Dallas Red' is hardier than many and grows quickly; it bears dark red blooms. 'Muskogee' grows vigorously; mid-lavender flowers. 'Natchez' is white-flowered. 'Seminole' is compact, to 10ft (3m), with midpink flowers. 'Tuscarora' has coral-pink flowers.
◻ ◊ **Z7–9** H 25ft (8m)

Laurus nobilis
(Bay laurel, Sweet bay)
Evergreen, broadly conical tree, popular for its strongly aromatic foliage, used in cooking. The yellow-leaved 'Aurea' is slower growing, reaching about 25ft (8m).
◻ ◊ **Z8–10** H 40ft (12m)

Ligustrum lucidum
(Chinese privet)
Evergreen, broadly conical tree. Bold foliage is enhanced in late summer and autumn by large clusters of tiny white flowers, followed by small, blue-black fruits. It has two variegated forms that are smaller, to about 25ft (8m): 'Excelsum Superbum', with yellow-margined foliage; and 'Tricolor', which has pink-edged leaves when young, turning creamy white.
◻ ◊ **Z8–10** H 15m (50ft)

Luma apiculata
(syn. *Myrtus luma*)
This evergreen tree is best in areas where winters are mild. Rounded to spreading, it has glossy, aromatic foliage, cinnamon-brown bark that peels to leave creamy white patches, and white flowers in summer and autumn.
◻ ◊ **Z9-10** H 30ft (10m) or more

LIGUSTRUM LUCIDUM 'EXCELSUM SUPERBUM'

M

Maackia amurensis

This makes a small, rounded and spreading deciduous tree, with dark green, divided leaves, gray when they first open. The small white, or slightly blue-tinged, fragrant pealike flowers appear in dense, upright spikes in mid- to late summer and are followed by flattened seed-pods. Grows best in areas with hot summers.
🌣 ◊ Z5–7 H 25ft (8m)

Maytenus boaria

(Mayten)
Variably shaped evergreen tree or shrub with upright or hanging branches bearing fine-toothed, glossy, dark green, elongate leaves. Small clusters of pale green, tubular flowers in spring are followed by orange-red fruit with red seeds. Both males and females are needed for fruit.
🌣 ◊ Z9–10 H 30ft (10m)

Morus alba

(White mulberry)
Deciduous, spreading tree with heart-shaped, bright green leaves that turn yellow in autumn. It bears insipid-tasting white fruits in late summer. 'Pendula' is an excellent form for small gardens. It makes a mound of weeping shoots, arching to the ground with bright green foliage, sometimes reaching 15ft (5m) tall and across. It is especially attractive when bearing its small but striking, edible red fruits along the drooping branches.
🌣 ◊ Z4–8 H 30ft (10m)

MAGNOLIA

Unrivaled in the size and spectacle of their usually fragrant flowers, magnolias are splendid trees. Some kinds, such as *M. denudata* (Yulan) and *M. obovata* (syn. *M. hypoleuca*), need acidic soil.
🌣 ◊ Z6–9 except where stated

Spring-flowering magnolias
For large white flowers, try *M. denudata* (Yulan), or the more upright *M. kobus* (Z5–9) and *M. salicifolia* (*p.25*). All grow to about 30ft (10m).

M. 'Galaxy', to 25ft (8m), has big purple-pink flowers, and *M.* 'Heaven Scent', 30ft (10m), has goblet-shaped pink flowers.

Forms of *M.* × *loebneri* (Z5–9) reach about 25ft (8m). Among the best are 'Leonard Messel', with starry pink flowers, and 'Merrill', with profuse white flowers.

The many cultivars of *M.* × *soulangeana* (Z5–9, *p.18*) include 'Brozzonii' (white flowers) and 'Picture' (rich purple-pink and white flowers). Both are 25ft (8m).

MAGNOLIA × SOULANGEANA

MAGNOLIA GRANDIFLORA 'GOLIATH'

Summer-flowering magnolias
M. macrophylla grows to 30ft (10m) or more. It is broadly conical with huge leaves and large but often sparse, creamy white flowers. *M. obovata* (syn. *M. hypoleuca*, Z5–9) also reaches 30ft (10m) or more. It has bold leaves and fragrant, crimson-centered flowers, often followed by red fruits in autumn. *M. virginiana* is usually smaller, with smaller flowers and glossy green leaves, blue-white beneath; var. *australis* is evergreen in favorable areas.

Evergreen magnolias
The evergreen magnolias have bold foliage and late flowers in summer and autumn. *M. delavayi* (Z7–9), to 25ft (8m), has large deep blue-green leaves and big, creamy white flowers. *M. grandiflora* (Z7–9), a large tree where it is native but usually less than 30ft (10m) in colder areas, has glossy dark green leaves and large, fragrant white flowers in summer. 'Edith Bogue' is particularly hardy; 'Goliath' has broad leaves and very large flowers.

MALUS (CRABAPPLE)

Ornamental crabapples provide some of the toughest of all flowering trees, growing in any reasonable soil. They are quite hardy and capable of withstanding a good deal of exposure. In addition, they provide a profusion of flowers in late spring and early summer, often followed by variously colored ornamental fruits. They are deciduous with a rounded to spreading habit, unless otherwise stated, and are ideal specimen trees for small gardens.

▨ ◊ Z5–8 except where indicated H 25ft (8m)

Crabapples grown for flowers and fruit
Most crabapples are grown for their attractive flowers, which are often fragrant, and for their fruits.

M. 'Butterball' has pink flowers on arching branches, followed by very profuse and persistent rounded fruits, which mature from yellow flushed with red to gold. M. 'Donald Wyman' has white flowers from pink buds and small, glossy red fruits. M. floribunda (Japanese crabapple, Z4–8) is compact with masses of flowers, red in bud opening to pale pink and eventually white, followed later by small yellow, slender-stalked fruits.
M. 'Golden Hornet' (pp.8, 23) has white flowers

from pink buds and showy golden yellow fruits.
M. hupehensis is vigorous, to 30ft (10m) or more, with large white flowers from pink buds, and small, cherrylike red fruits. M. 'Indian Magic' bears red buds opening to rose-pink flowers, followed by long-lasting, glossy red fruit that become orange.
M. 'Jewelberry', to 15ft (5m) bears masses of white flowers opening from pink buds at an early age. Glossy red fruit follow. M. 'John Downie' is broadly conical. The pink buds opening to white flowers are followed by very distinctive, conical red fruits flushed with yellow. M. 'Red Sentinel' (p.9) is broadly conical, with white flowers and persistent glossy red fruits. M. 'Snowdrift' is compact with white flowers from pink buds and small, persistent, glossy orange-red fruits. M. transitoria has elegant foliage, small white flowers, and yellow, pea-sized fruits as the leaves turn yellow.

Crabapples grown for foliage
Some of the crabapples are grown particularly for their purple foliage. As with other purple-leaved trees, they color best in full sun. M. 'Liset' has bronze-green leaves and purple-pink flowers in late spring followed by small purple-red fruits. M. 'Profusion' (Z4–8) has bronze-purple leaves, red when young, later dark green, deep purple-pink flowers, and red-purple fruits. M. 'Royalty' has deep red-purple foliage, keeping its color well and turning red in autumn. The flowers are red-purple, followed by small, deep purple fruits.

Crabapples grown for habit
Several crabapples combine ornamental flowers and fruit with an attractive habit.

MALUS
'JOHN DOWNIE'

MALUS
FLORIBUNDA

M. 'Red Jade' (p.60), to 12ft (4m), has a mushroom-shaped head of arching shoots with pink-tinged, white flowers, then glossy red fruits. M. 'Royal Beauty' is smaller, weeping, with purple leaves and deep red-purple flowers. M. sargentii grows only 6–10ft (2–3m) tall and bears profuse white flowers and dark red fruit.
M. tschonoskii (p.15) is broadly columnar, to about 30ft (10m). It has bright orange and red autumn color, small white flowers, tinged pink, and yellow fruits, flushed red.

MALUS 'SNOWDRIFT'

Nyssa sinensis

N

Nyssa sinensis
(Chinese tupelo)
This deciduous tree provides color at least as good as the better-known *N. sylvatica* on a tree only half the size. It has large, dark green leaves, which turn to brilliant shades of orange, red, and yellow in autumn. Often on several stems, it has a rounded to spreading habit. Requires acidic soil.
⊠ ◊ Z7–9 H 30ft (10m)

O

Ostrya virginiana
(American hop hornbeam, Ironwood)
This deciduous, conical to spreading tree bears toothed, dark green leaves; usually little autumn color. Showy, light green, 2in (5cm) conelike fruit clusters turn brown in autumn. Good as a specimen tree. Often tolerant of dry, stony soil and can make an attractive street tree.
⊠ ◊ Z5–9 H 30ft (10m)

Oxydendrum arboreum
(Sorrel tree, Sourwood)
A deciduous, broadly conical tree, sometimes shrubby. In autumn, its long bold, glossy dark green leaves turn to shades of purple, yellow, and red. Large, arching clusters of small, urn-shaped white flowers are produced in late summer and early autumn. It is best grown in acidic soil.
⊠ ◊ Z5–9 H 30ft (10m)

P

Photinia
These deciduous or evergreen, mostly broadly columnar trees are often grown for their attractive leaves. They also produce white flowers, followed by colorful fruits. *P. davidiana*, (Z7–9) 25ft (8m) tall, is evergreen and shrubby, with arching branches. Bright red fruits follow clusters of small white flowers in summer and may persist well into winter, when occasional leaves turn bright red before they fall. The main ornamental feature of the smaller evergreen *P.* × *fraseri*

Oxydendrum arboreum

Photinia × *fraseri*
'Red Robin'

(Z8–9), 20ft (6m) tall, is its young foliage, but it will often produce small white flowers in mid- and late spring; '**Birmingham**', '**Red Robin**', and '**Robusta**' are good forms with bright red young leaves. The even smaller *P. villosa*, (Z4–9) 15ft (5m) tall, is deciduous and rounded to spreading, sometimes shrubby, and needs acidic soil. It has dark green leaves, bronze when young and turning bright orange-red in autumn. Hawthornlike white flowers are borne in late spring, followed by small, bright red fruits.
⊠ ◊

Picea pungens
(Colorado spruce)
Best known in its blue-leaved forms, such as **f.** *glauca* (*p.26, 35*) or '**Koster**', this evergreen conifer has thick shoots, densely covered in rigid, sharp-tipped, bright silvery blue needles. It is best grown in acidic soil and is narrowly columnar in shape.
⊠ ◊ Z3–8 H 50ft (15m)

PRUNUS (CHERRIES, ALMONDS, PLUMS)

The cherries, almonds, and plums provide us with some of the best-loved spring-flowering trees. Most are small and rounded to spreading in habit; some provide additional interest, such as good autumn color or attractive bark.

🏵 ◊ Z6–8 except where indicated H 25–30ft (8–10m)

Flowering cherries

Some excellent early-flowering cherries include *P.* 'Okame' (Z5–8), rich pink, with good autumn color; and *P.* 'Pandora' pale pink, with bronze young leaves. *P. sargentii* (Z5–9) has rich pink flowers and bronze young leaves, red in autumn. *P.* × *subhirtella* 'Stellata' has pale pink flowers with pointed, starlike petals.

There are some semi-double-flowered cherries, including *P.* 'Accolade' and the long-flowering, shrubby *P.* 'Hally Jolivette' (*p.7*), to 15ft (5m); both are pale pink.

Double-flowered forms include *P.* × *subhirtella* 'Autumnalis' (white, pink-tinged in bud, *p.21*) and

'Autumnalis Rosea' (pink), both of which flower in autumn and early spring.

Japanese cherries

Recommended pink Japanese cherries include *P.* 'Kanzan' (double, deep pink) and *P.* 'Pink Perfection' (bright pink in large clusters). Recommended white-flowered forms include *P.* 'Mount Fuji' (syn. *P.* 'Shirotae', double) and *P.* 'Taihaku' (Great white cherry), with very large flowers.

The very late *P.* 'Shirofugen' has double flowers with purple-pink buds opening to white, then fading to purple-pink again amid bronze young foliage. *P.* 'Ukon' has semi-double, creamy flowers, flushed green and pink.

Cherries grown for bark

P. maackii (Manchurian cherry, Z3–7) has golden brown peeling bark and small white flowers in spring; 'Amber Beauty' has amber bark. *P. serrula* (Tibetan cherry, *p.23*) has glossy, mahogany red bark and white flowers.

Cherries for ornamental habit

Good upright cherries include the narrowly columnar *P.* 'Amanogawa', with single to semidouble, pink flowers, and *P. sargentii* RANCHO (Z5–9), with pink flowers and good autumn color. The broadly columnar *P.* 'Spire' has pink flowers and attractive orange and red autumn color.

There are also a number of weeping forms: *P.* 'Kiku-shidare-zakura' (syn. *P.* 'Cheal's Weeping') reaches only 8ft (2.5m), and has clusters of large, double pink flowers. *P. pendula* (*p.37*) has slender pendulous shoots. Good pink forms include 'Pendula Rosea' (*p.14*) and

the double 'Pendula Rubra'. *P.* × *yedoensis* has arching branches, to 20ft (6m), and an attractive mass of pale pink flowers, fading to white, in early spring.

Almonds and plums

Forms of *P. cerasifera* (Cherry plum, Z5–9) have purple foliage, but their small, profuse flowers, borne in early spring, pink in 'Nigra', white in 'Pissardii', are their best asset. *P. dulcis* (Almond, Z5–8) has very early, large, pink or white flowers. *P. mume* (Japanese apricot) has forms that produce attractive white to deep pink flowers in early spring.

PRUNUS 'UKON'

PRUNUS × SUBHIRTELLA 'STELLATA'

PRUNUS SARGENTII

PINUS DENSIFLORA
'UMBRACULIFERA'

Pinus

Pines are evergreen conifers.
P. bungeana (Lacebark pine, **Z4–7**) has bark that flakes, leaving a patchwork of cream, gray, and green. It is slow growing, columnar or bushy headed, and may reach 30ft (10m). *P. densiflora* 'Umbraculifera' (**Z4–7**) makes a dense, rounded head of slender gray-green needles. Forms of *P. sylvestris* (Scots pine, **Z3–7**) include **'Aurea'**, with bright yellow winter foliage, which may exceed 30ft (10m). **'Fastigiata'** is narrow, to 25ft (8m) tall; **'Watereri'** is rounded, with blue-gray foliage, to nearly 30ft (10m).
◫ ◊

Pittosporum tenuifolium

Evergreen, broadly columnar tree (*p.35*) with small, wavy-edged leaves on dark shoots. Deep purple-red, honey-scented flowers open in late spring and early summer. **'Abbotsbury Gold'** has leaves blotched yellow-green in the center; **'Purpureum'** has glossy purple foliage; **'Silver Queen'** has gray-green, white-edged leaves; and

'Warnham Gold' has pale green leaves, soft yellow in winter.
◫ ◊ **Z9–10** H 30ft (10m)

Pseudocydonia sinensis

Unusual deciduous tree grown for its deeply ridged trunk and mottled bark in shades of green, brown, and gray. Pink flowers in spring and large, oval yellow fruit in autumn add interest.
◫ ◊ **Z6–8** H 20ft (6m)

Pterostyrax hispida

(Epaulette tree)
Spreading, deciduous, often multistemmed tree with large, pale green leaves and showy clusters of fragrant, hanging white flowers in summer. May be short lived.
◫ ◊ **Z5–8** H 30ft (10m)

Pyrus calleryana

'Chanticleer' (Pear)
Narrow and fast-growing, deciduous tree with glossy foliage, red-purple in late autumn and winter. Small white flowers appear in late winter and early spring, and small russet-brown fruits may be produced in autumn.
◫ ◊ **Z5–8** H 30ft (10m)

PITTOSPORUM TENUIFOLIUM

ROBINIA 'IDAHO'

Pyrus salicifolia 'Pendula'

(Weeping silver pear)
This deciduous tree (*p.21*) makes a mound of pendulous shoots bearing silvery gray, willowlike leaves. Creamy white flowers open in spring.
◫ ◊ **Z5–9** H 15ft (5m)

Q

Quercus

(Oak)
Several small evergreen oaks make valuable foliage plants. *Q. glauca* (**Z8–9**) is broadly columnar and bushy, to about 20ft (6m) tall, with red buds and glossy green leaves, bronze in spring. *Q. myrsinifolia* (**Z7–9**) is rounded, with dark green, taper-pointed leaves, bronze when young. *Q. phillyreoides* (**Z7–9**) is an often shrubby tree with leathery dark green leaves.
◫ ◊ H 30ft (10m)

R

Rhus chinensis 'September Beauty' (Sumac)

Deciduous, rounded to

broadly columnar tree, with leaves that turn orange-red in autumn and clusters of small, creamy white flowers in late summer and early autumn.
🏵 ◊ Z5–8 H 20ft (6m)

Robinia
These are often thorny trees. **R. 'Idaho'** (**Z6–10**) is spreading, to 40ft (12m), with fragrant flowers in late spring. Avoid most forms of the common **R. pseudoacacia** (**Z4–9**) if you want a small tree (golden-leaved **'Frisia'** reaches at least 50ft/15m). However, the more compact **'Umbraculifera'** (Mop-headed locust), grown for its dense rounded head, will reach only about 20ft (6m).
🏵 ◊

S

Salix
(Willow)
There are several willows that are suitable for growing in small gardens (vigorous kinds should be planted far from buildings, since their invasive root systems can damage drains). Forms of **S. alba** (White willow, **Z4–9**), such as **'Britzensis'** (*p.57*) and **subsp. vitellina**, are grown for their colored winter stems. Pollard them for brighter shoots and to keep them small (*see p.57*). **S. babylonica 'Tortuosa'** (Dragon's claw willow, **Z6–9**), to 28ft (9m), has twisted stems. **S. caprea 'Kilmarnock'** (**Z6–8**) is 6ft (2m) or less. Thick shoots weep almost to the ground and, in late winter to spring, they bear silvery catkins that turn yellow as the stamens emerge.

SORBUS (MOUNTAIN ASH)

This genus is often broadly divided into two groups, the whitebeams and the mountain ashes. Both provide a good range of small deciduous trees offering white flowers, attractive berries in many colors, and often excellent autumn color.
🏵 ◊ **Hardiness varies**
H 30ft (10m)

SORBUS ALNIFOLIA

Whitebeams
The whitebeams, mostly rounded to spreading, have toothed or lobed leaves. They are mostly tough trees, good in dry soils and urban sites. **S. alnifolia** (Korean mountain ash, **Z5–8**) is conical, later rounded, sometimes up to 60ft (20m), with leaves orange to red in autumn, and red berries. **S. aria** (**Z6–8**) has glossy dark green leaves and red berries; **'Lutescens'** has silvery young foliage. **S. intermedia** (**Z6–8**) is dense and rounded and is slightly larger than *S. aria*; it has dark green leaves and bright red fruits. **S. × thuringiaca 'Fastigiata'** (**Z5–8**) is similar to *S. aria* but is dense and broadly conical.

Mountain ashes
These are broadly conical and more graceful than the whitebeams, with leaves cut

SORBUS SCALARIS

into numerous leaflets. They generally prefer a moister soil and include the best species for autumn color. **S. americana** (American mountain ash, **Z3–8**) has clusters of red berries, and yellow or red autumn foliage. **S. aucuparia** (European mountain ash, **Z4–7**, *p.31*) is similar, with forms such as **'Fructu Luteo'**, with yellow berries. **S. cashmiriana** (**Z5–7**) is a small tree, to 25ft (8m) tall, with elegant foliage and white or pink flowers and large white berries, pink when immature. **S. commixta** (**Z6–8**) has red autumn color and bright orange-red fruits. **S. hupehensis** (**Z6–8**), to 25ft (8m), is among the best for white fruits, with blue-green leaves, red in autumn; **var. obtusa** has pink berries. **S. 'Joseph Rock'** (**Z7–8**) is broadly columnar and produces yellow fruits and orange, red, and purple autumn color. **S. sargentiana** (**Z5–7**) has bold leaves, red in autumn, and large heads of small red berries. **S. scalaris** (**Z6–8**) is spreading, with fernlike foliage, purple in autumn, and red berries. **S. vilmorinii** (**Z6–8**) is smaller, reaching only 15ft (5m) tall, and produces red berries that turn pink, then white.

S. 'Erythroflexuosa' (Z5–9) is a rounded to spreading, deciduous tree, to 15ft (5m) tall, with contorted shoots, bright orange-pink in winter. *S. integra* 'Hakuro-nishiki' (Z6–8, *p.15*) is a rounded to spreading, deciduous shrub, usually grown as a dwarf tree, to 5ft (1.5m) tall. It has white young foliage that becomes speckled with dark green.
◨ ◊

Sophora japonica 'Pendula'
(Japanese pagoda tree)
This weeping, deciduous tree has a dense head of twisted branches, from which long hanging shoots cascade to the ground. Slightly fragrant, white pea flowers open in late summer, but rarely, and only at the end of very hot summers.
◨ ◊ Z5–9 H 10ft (3m) or more

Stewartia
These are deciduous or evergreen trees grown for their attractive white flowers, often peeling bark, and good autumn color. They require acidic soil. *S. ovata*, 15ft (5m) tall, is often shrubby, with large white flowers in

STYRAX JAPONICUS

SYRINGA RETICULATA

summer. The young leaves are red, then green, turning red once again in autumn. The larger *S. pseudocamellia* 30ft (10m) tall, is broadly columnar with large white flowers in midsummer. Older trunks have red-brown, tan, and gray peeling bark. The dark green leaves turn shades of orange and red in autumn.
◨ ◊ Z5–8

Styrax
These graceful deciduous or evergreen trees produce fragrant, pendulous flowers. *S. japonicus* (Japanese snowbell, *p.10*) is rounded to spreading, 25ft (8m) tall, and needs acidic soil. Bell-shaped white flowers hang on slender stalks in early summer. Glossy green leaves turn yellow or red in autumn. 'Pink Chimes' produces pale pink flowers. *S. obassia* (Fragrant snowbell) is more upright and is also larger, to 25ft (12m) tall. It has bold, rounded leaves and drooping spikes of white flowers in early and midsummer. Does best in acidic soil.
◉ ◊ Z6–8

Syringa reticulata
(Japanese tree lilac)
Deciduous, rounded to spreading tree, which bears small fragrant white flowers opening in large heads in summer. 'Ivory Lace' is compact and free-flowering.
◨ ◊ Z4–7 H 30ft (10m)

Syringa vulgaris
(Common lilac)
This spreading shrub may become treelike with age. It bears heart-shaped leaves and very fragrant single or double lilac flowers in late spring and early summer.
◨ ◊ Z4–8 H 22ft (7m)

T

Taxus baccata
(English yew)
Evergreen, rounded to spreading conifer with dark green foliage and purple-brown bark. 'Dovastonii Aurea' is male, to about 15ft (5m) tall but wide-spreading, with drooping shoots and leaves with yellow edges. 'Fastigiata' (Irish yew) is female, with dense upright

THUJA KORAIENSIS

shoots and red fruits.
'Fastigiata Aureomarginata' is also upright but is male and grows only to 15ft (5m), and has yellow-edged leaves. 'Standishii', to 5ft (1.5m), is a miniature selection of 'Fastigiata', with yellow leaves. The foliage and seeds of all yews are toxic.
☀ ◊ **Z7–8** H 30ft (10m)

Thuja koraiensis
(Korean arborvitae)
A dense, bushy, shrubby or narrowly conical, slow-growing tree with dark green aromatic foliage, bright silvery white beneath.
▨ ◊ **Z5–7** H 30ft (10m)

Thuja occidentalis
(Eastern arborvitae)
This small, narrowly columnar evergreen conifer with scalelike leaves has several forms: 'Europa Gold', with bright yellow foliage; 'Holmstrup', which is compact with vertical sprays of rich green foliage; and 'Smaragd', which is slow growing and narrow, with bright green foliage.
▨ ◊ **Z2–7** H 20ft (6m)

TRACHYCARPUS FORTUNEI

Trachycarpus fortunei
(Chinese windmill palm, Chusan palm)
Evergreen, narrowly columnar tree with large leaves deeply cut into long, slender lobes and borne in a cluster on an unbranched fibrous trunk. Large clusters of tiny creamy flowers emerge in early summer.
▣ ◊ **Z9–10** H 30ft (10m)

Trochodendron aralioides
Evergreen, broadly columnar tree with leathery dark green, taper-pointed leaves and clusters of bright green flowers at the ends of the shoots in spring. This unusual specimen is suitable for a woodland garden, and it requires acidic soil to thrive.
▣☀ ◊ **Z6–10** H 30ft (10m)

Tsuga heterophylla
'Laursen's Column'
This evergreen conifer, a form of the normally large Western hemlock, has a narrowly columnar habit, making it excellent as a specimen tree. The dark green leaves have white bands beneath. It grows well in sun or shade in most soils, including alkaline.
☀▣ **Z6–8** H 25ft (8m)

U

Ulmus
(Elm)
Deciduous trees, grown mainly for their foliage and habit. Some forms are excellent for small gardens. *U. glabra* 'Camperdownii' (Camperdown elm, **Z5–7**), 25ft (8m) tall, makes a dense mound of shoots, weeping to the ground. Produces twisted branches

and toothed, matte, dark green leaves. *Ulmus minor* 'Dampieri Aurea' (**Z5–8**), 30ft (10m) tall, is broadly conical, with golden leaves.
▨

V

Viburnum prunifolium
(Black haw)
An upright, broadly columnar deciduous tree, sometimes shrubby, with dark green leaves often turning orange or red in autumn. Domed heads of white flowers in late spring are followed by pink, later blue-black, fruits.
▣ ◊ **Z3–9** H 15ft (5m)

Viburnum sieboldii
Compact and spreading, large deciduous shrub that may be trained as a tree by removing the lower branches as it develops to give a clear stem. It has bold, glossy dark green leaves and produces large heads of small white flowers in late spring, later followed by glossy red fruits that turn black.
▣▣ ◊ **Z5–8** H 20ft (6m)

VIBURNUM PRUNIFOLIUM

INDEX

DEC - 2000

ACKNOWLEDGMENTS

Picture research Emily Hedges

Index Hilary Bird

Illustrations Karen Cochrane

Dorling Kindersley would like to thank:
All staff at the RHS, in particular Susanne
Mitchell, Karen Wilson, and Barbara Haynes
at Vincent Square; Sir Harold Hillier Gardens
and Arboretum; John Hillier; Helen Bracey,
Candida Frith-Macdonald, Anna Hayman and
Lesley Malkin for design and editorial help.

American Horticultural Society
Visit AHS at www.ahs.org or call them at
1-800-777-7931 ext. 10. Membership benefits
include *The American Gardener* magazine,
free admission to flower shows, the free seed
exchange, book services, and the Gardener's
Information Service.

Photography
The publisher would like to thank the
following for their kind permission to
reproduce their photographs:
(key: t=top; b=below; l=left; r=right)

Dr. Mike Dirr: 67bl
Garden Picture Library: Mark Bolton 40;
John Glover 10l (Valley Gardens, Windsor),
13; Jerry Pavia 30; J.S. Sira 37l (The Coppice,
Surrey)
John Glover: 8bl (Old Place Farm, Kent), 22b,
25tr, 29t
Jerry Harpur: 10r (Helen Yemm), 26r, 31t, 34
(Little Malvern Court)
Marcus Harpur: 22t
Andrew Lawson: 21b, 28r, 41
Marianne Majerus: 18r (designer: Penny
Snell), 36 (designer: Tessa Hobbs)
S&O Mathews: 8tr, 9, 11, 14, 15r, 32, 33
Clive Nichols: 12, 15l (The Dingle, Welshpool,
Wales), 16 (Osler Road, Oxford), 17t, 17b
(designer: C. Caplin), 18l (White Windows,
Hampshire), 19 (Little Court, Crawley,
Hampshire), 20 (designer: Jill Billington), 21t
(The Anchorage, Kent), 23t and b, 35bl
(designer: Thomasina Tarling), 38t (Ling
Beeches, Yorkshire), 39 (designers: Mr. and
Mrs. D. Terry)

Cover photography:
S&O Mathews: back tl; **Clive Nichols:** back b;
Jerry Harpur: front tl; **S&O Mathews:** front r